Palms of the Fiji Islands

Dick Watling

Illustrated by

George Bennett

ENVIRONMENTAL CONSULTANTS FIJI

USP Library Cataloguing-in-Publication Data

Watling, Dick

Palms of Fiji / Dick Watling. – Suva, Fiji : Environmental Consultants, 2005.

p. : col. ill. ; cm.

ISBN 982-9047-02-4

1. Palms–Fiji 2. Palms–Fiji–Identification 3. Palms–Protection–Fiji 4. Palms–Propagation–Fiji I. Title.

QK495.P17W27 2005   584.5099611

First edition published 2005 by Environmental Consultants (Fiji) Ltd.

Design and Cover by Heather Lee.

Typeset in Adobe Garamond, URW Egyptienne and Fruitiger.

Artwork and production by Streamline Creative Ltd, Auckland, New Zealand.

Printed in China through Colorcraft Ltd, Hong Kong.

All orders should be placed with: Environmental Consultants (Fiji) Ltd.,

PO Box 2041, Government Buildings, Suva, Fiji.

Email: watling@connect.com.fj

Website: www.environmentfiji.com

For people who love plants

Acknowledgements

It is always difficult to know where or how to begin when writing acknowledgements. In the Preface I have written of the significant roles of Elsa and David Miller, and the late Dick Phillips, without whom this book would never have been written. The same can be extended to George Bennett, for if he had not become involved, I doubt if I would have attempted to write the text. As my friends keep reminding me, my photography is legendary – for all the wrong reasons, so being able to work with an artist of George Bennett's calibre was a windfall. More so, because George happens to be a very interested and knowledgeable palm enthusiast with green fingers, when they are not painting. So George was able to make much better use of the material that I provided for his illustrations, than I could have dared to hope for. As everyone can readily see, this book is a collaborative effort and it would be very thin indeed without George's contribution.

If Dylan Fuller had not completed his Master's Degree on the palms of Fiji, I doubt I could have written the book, because his work provided a rigorous scientific review of our palms. Dylan was also very generous in answering a plethora of questions, providing much advice, as well as some photographs for me to work from. This book is in no small measure a scion of Dylan's dedicated work and enthusiasm for palms. It is such a shame that he now has to work in London!

Paul Geraghty provided most if not all of the Fijian language content of this book and commented and corrected my own contributions and the tangled record of 'recorded names' by a variety of botanists in times gone by. Paul also provided critical and fascinating information on the linguistic trail of our *Pritchardia* fan palms and the *Metroxylon*-sago palm puzzle. Much of this could not be included in the book, but it was sufficient for me to believe that there is as good, if not better, linguistic evidence for *Pritchardia pacifica* being a Fijian palm, than there is other evidence for its not being a Fijian palm.

Ian Rolls orchestrated the distribution maps and other technical illustrations, while also providing a useful sounding-board for many diverse issues. His kava preparation does not improve but he still manages to procure a visa to drink it on almost any occasion. David Zundel of the Garden of the Sleeping Giant provided me with a copy of Dick Phillips' lists and manuscripts, enabling a chapter on cultivation to be attributed to Dick. He also gave useful criticisms on an early draft.

I am very grateful to a large number of people who generously provided information, material or in other ways assisted in the preparation of this book, including Art Whistler, Baravi Thaman, Isaac Rounds, Marika Tuiwawa, Gunnar Keppel, Vili Masibalavu, Tevita Kete, Sikeli Cabenalevu, Joerg Kretzschmar, Craig Morley, Geoff Taylor (sorry you sank out of your depth while trying to photograph those sago palms for me), John Dransfield, Bill Baker, Di Swavely, Heather Lee, Aisake Tale, Jeff Marcus, Will McClatchey, Timoci Bulitavu, David Olson, Linda Farley and the Wildlife Conservation Society, Kolinio Moce, Napolioni Batimala, Robbie Stone, Max Storck, Peceli Tuisawau and the Namaqumaqua community, Ratu Iliesa Tiqe Saukitoga and Master Koto. Paul Geraghty, Kim Gravelle, Elsa Miller and Guy Dutson all helped with comments on the manuscript and I am grateful to Tim Chamberlain for editorial assistance. Murray and Shirley Charters provided their usual encouragement from afar. The portrait of Dick Phillips is reproduced with the permission of his niece, Di Swavely.

The isoheyetal rainfall maps are reproduced with modification from Gale, I.N. 1991. *Hydrogeological Maps of Viti Levu and Vanua Levu*. Mineral Resources Department, Suva. The Wildlife Conservation Society, SOPAC and Forestry Department are gratefully acknowledged for the forest cover basemap.

My wife Kelera would prefer I planted more palms than hide in the office writing about them, but with Fay and Colin, she graciously put up with my frequent absence from family duties – something I will now need to redress!

Foreword

The idea of this book arose from the frustration of trying to find out about Pacific palms for landscaping purposes. As a landscape architect in Fiji, I was faced with the availability in plant nurseries of many exotic (foreign) plants and few endemic or native plants for gardens here. The resultant gardens look like tropical gardens similar to those found throughout the tropical world rather than specifically Fijian ones.

There is so little known about endemic Fijian plants. What is known is usually in botanical books, written for people with botanical training and not accessible to or understood by the general public.

Native Fijian palms are precious. Some have only recently been discovered by the botanical world and some are probably still waiting to be found by botanists, to be "identified" and "described". Many are highly endangered.

These beautiful and varied palms are mainly rainforest dwellers, and by bringing them "into the light" in this book, we hope to raise awareness of some of Fiji's "national treasures" so that conservation efforts can safeguard them from extinction. It is important for the Fiji Government or the University of the South Pacific to establish a live seed bank of these endangered species that would be available for nurseries to propagate for future generations.

Endangered animals are considered much more important than endangered plants. Endangered plants go silently into extinction – no one knows when this happens and few seem to care. This could easily happen to many of the palms in this book.

Palms are the regal elements of tropical gardens. The Pacific and Fiji islands have some of the rarest species of palms in the world. I am fortunate to have friends who share my passion for these.

I would like to thank my husband David for his support of this book.

Dr Dick Watling has a profound knowledge of Fiji's environment. He knows where these palms grow and the uncertain future for them and the forest habitats where they survive.

George Bennett, an artist with an international reputation, has illustrated many of Fiji's stamps, mainly with a natural history theme. We decided on painted illustrations as they reveal more detail and character than photographs. George's illustrations show the palms in their natural environment.

To the graphic wizard, Ian Rolls, thank you for the wonderful distribution maps.

We all pay tribute to the late Dick Phillips who has inspired us all with his love of palms and his lifelong work in the public and private gardens of Fiji, and in bringing these relatively unknown palms to public knowledge.

And thank you, palms, for being there – we always enjoy your presence.

Elsa Miller
Suva, Fiji
June 2005

Contents

Acknowledgements   4

Foreword   6

Preface   10

Introduction   13

    Palms   14

    The Purpose of this Book   16

    Scope   16

    The Species Accounts   16

    The Illustrations   18

    The Distribution Maps   18

    Access to Wild Growing Palms   18

Fiji: The Country, Vegetation and the Palm Flora   19

    The Fiji Islands   20

    Fiji's Flora and Vegetation   22

    Fiji's Palm Flora   28

        Overview   28

        Relationships   29

        Diversity and Distribution 29

        Dispersal   32

    Conservation   37

        The Forests and Forestry   37

        Protected Areas   40

        Conservation Threat Status of Fiji's Palms 40

        Conservation Synopsis 42

Species Accounts: Fiji's Indigenous Palms   45

    Alsmithia longipes   46

    Balaka longirostris   50

    Balaka macrocarpa   54

    Balaka microcarpa   58

    Balaka seemannii   62

    Balaka streptostachys   66

    Balaka 'bulitavu'   70

Balaka 'natewa' 72

Calamus vitiensis 74

Clinostigma exorrhizum 78

Cyphosperma tanga 82

Cyphosperma trichospadix 86

Cyphosperma 'naboutini' 89

Heterospathe phillipsii 92

Hydriastele boumae 98

Hydriastele vitiensis 102

Metroxylon vitiense 108

Neoveitchia storckii 112

Physokentia petiolatus 118

Physokentia thurstonii 120

Pritchardia pacifica 122

Pritchardia thurstonii 126

Veitchia filifera 130

Veitchia joannis 134

Veitchia simulans 138

Veitchia vitiensis 140

Naturalised Palms in Fiji – Ancient Introductions 146

Coconut – *Cocos nucifera* 146

Sago Palm – *Metroxylon warburgii* 151

Naturalised Palms in Fiji – Recent Introductions 153

Betel Nut Palm – *Areca catechu* 153

Date Palm – *Phoenix dactylifera* 154

Ivory Cane Palm – *Pinanga coronata* 156

MacArthur Palm – *Ptychosperma macarthurii* 156

Propagation and Culture of Fiji's Native Palms

by Dick Phillips 159

References 177

Glossary 181

Index 185

Preface

Many will wonder what a birdwatcher is doing writing a book on palms. My only excuse is that I was asked to write it. The genesis and fruition of this book is attributable solely to Elsa Miller. It was her idea; she was the first to connect it with the artistic talents of George Bennett, and it is Elsa and David Miller's philanthropy which has enabled the project to proceed to publication.

For my own part, if I had not had the good fortune of knowing the late Dick Phillips and from his generosity and enthusiasm developed an interest in palms, then I certainly would never have considered writing the book. My interest in Fiji's palms developed because Dick Phillips gave me some to grow in my Tamavua garden, teaching me all his seed germination methods and anything else I wanted to know. His enthusiasm was highly infectious, but to start with I may have been something of a disappointment to him. This is because I was not interested in any palm; it had to be Fijian palms or, at a stretch, those from other tropical Pacific islands. Dick found this uncomfortably narrow-minded but was prepared to overlook this as I provided him with some palm seeds from various parts of Fiji and, perhaps more importantly, showed that the palms he gave me grew and were well looked after.

I soon realised what a truly remarkable group of plants the Fijian palms are and how they encapsulated issues of island flora biogeography and conservation challenges. They were all endemic to Fiji (arguably at least), astonishingly restricted ranges were prevalent, while over half were highly endangered.

The plight of Fiji's palms is a microcosm of the plight of Fiji's forests which are being butchered and burned, year in and year out, without so much as a whimper. Palms are a very appropriate conservation flagship and also provide a wonderful opportunity for some of the more academic interests of the vulnerability of island floras and extinction processes. This was brought home to me as I sat watching three species of bird devour fruit of the then undescribed *Hydriastele boumae*. I knew well that those birds were great flyers and wanderers – even between islands – but this palm was restricted to a few kilometres square in northern Taveuni. I certainly don't have an answer even now.

It was while I was dabbling in landscape work that firstly, I met Elsa – a landscape architect – and secondly, became aware how ridiculous it was that 90 percent of our landscapes are comprised of exotic species, while we had much in Fiji that we could use (half of our native plants are endemic). Clearly, our palms become highly significant here, yet nobody, with the exception of Dick Phillips and now Elsa Miller, has shown much interest in them as living plants.

Hopefully, this book will generate an interest in our native palms and in their conservation, which is now a pressing issue. It is also to be hoped that their use in local landscapes will inspire a general interest in the Fijian landscape rather than the generic one we encounter in any tropical country we visit.

We need to find a way to take palms to their rightful custodians, the Fijian landowners. Unless their interest can be generated, then palm conservation and that of the forests where they are found will be just a dream. Not surprisingly, at this point in Fiji's history, landowners' interests are determined largely by income requirements. It is a great wrong that conservation of their forest by landowners is not a recognised land use, in fact it is a penalty. Generous subsidies are paid in the 'developed' world to those who put aside or restore native habitats, but in Fiji and elsewhere in developing countries, landowners are effectively penalised if they want to leave their forests as forest.

In acknowledging landowners, I am grateful to Bill Baker who, breaking with tradition, agreed to my request to have a new species of *Hydriastele* named for the people of Bouma on Taveuni where the palm is found. *Hydriastele boumae* is a fitting tribute to this community who have embarked on what is now an internationally recognised conservation programme for the forests of their vanua. The continued and long-term interest and support of the New Zealand Government in this venture, and that at Koroyanitu, needs special acknowledgement too.

Dick Watling
Suva, Fiji
June 2005

Introduction

Palms

For most of us in Fiji, the coconut has been a part of our life as far back as we can remember. Its many uses even today make it an important plant and there are few who are not aware of its significance to isolated island communities. We are not alone, for the coconut is the quintessential palm, the essence of the tropical world of sunshine, beaches and holidays in the minds of millions of people around the world. However, beyond the coconut, our knowledge diminishes rapidly, although as a group of plants with a characteristic appearance, most palms are readily recognised as such.

The vast majority of palms have a single stem and a crown of complex leaves. Neither the stem nor the leaves grow incrementally like standard trees. The distinctive crown remains similar throughout the life of the palm, other than increasing in height as the stem grows. Within this general uniformity, palms show great diversity. For instance, the Andean wax palm, *Ceroxylon* sp. is among the tallest trees in the world at up to 60m in height, while the diminutive lilliput palm, *Syagrus lilliputiana*, is only 10-15 cm tall at maturity. Most palms grow in rainforests, although a significant number grow in other habitats including open savanna, deserts, littoral forests, semi-aquatic freshwater, mangroves, limestone and ultrabasic rock habitats.

Quite a few palms are not single-trunked, but have multiple trunks growing as suckers from the base of the parent palm. Others appear to have no trunk, while a few have underground trunks. The only group which departs markedly from the general pattern are the liana-like rattans which have a very slender stem and which climb to and then over the canopy.

Palms generally bear large numbers of small, inconspicuous flowers. Collectively these can be colourful and in some cases fragrant, but these are exceptions. The fruits vary greatly in size, colour and number, from the size of a match head to twice the size of our largest coconuts.

Like grasses, palms are monocotyledons and it is currently estimated that there are about 2600 species in 210 genera. The numbers keep changing as taxonomists describe new species or change their minds over previously described species (refer page 28) to see how this has happened with Fiji's endemic palms).

Palm specialists have advanced terminology for all those parts of a palm that are necessary for all the specialised palm structures and comparative distinctions. In this book we will generally try to avoid the use of specialised terminology. Those requiring more detail could consult D.L. Jones, *Palms Throughout the World*, Reed New Holland, Sydney, 1995 or P.B. Tomlinson, *The Structural Biology of Palms*, Clarendon Press, Oxford, 1990. A glossary of terms is provided at the end of the book. Figure 1 (opposite page) provides the generalised palm structures as used in this book.

The Structure of a Palm

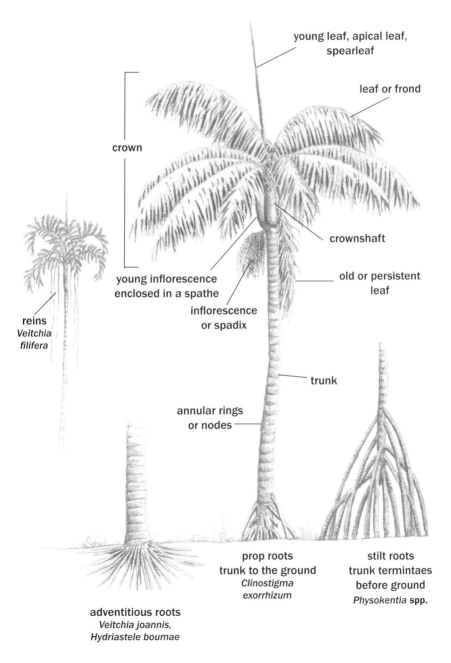

young leaf, apical leaf, spearleaf

leaf or frond

crown

crownshaft

young inflorescence enclosed in a spathe

old or persistent leaf

inflorescence or spadix

reins
Veitchia filifera

trunk

annular rings or nodes

prop roots
trunk to the ground
Clinostigma exorrhizum

stilt roots
trunk termintaes before ground
Physokentia **spp.**

adventitious roots
*Veitchia joannis,
Hydriastele boumae*

The Purpose of this Book

Fiji's 25 indigenous palms are a distinctive component of the country's natural heritage. With one and perhaps two exceptions they are all endemic to Fiji and over half of them are threatened with extinction and in desperate need of conservation management.

Fiji's palms are well known to palm specialists and academics throughout the world, yet in Fiji they are very poorly known. If we are to engage in effective conservation, these palms need to be much better known by the general public and not just by academics, conservationists and interested horticulturists. So this book has been written primarily for the general reader, especially residents of and visitors to Fiji, as well as for students and those interested in conservation and evolutionary biology of island communities. Fiji's palms have an interesting story to tell here.

Scope

This book covers the 31 known species of palm that may be found growing in the wild in Fiji. Of these, 24 are described, indigenous species; one is a presumed, but yet to be described indigenous species; two are introduced species of ancient origin and four are introduced species of relatively modern origin. These are not the only palms growing in Fiji; there are over 100 species of ornamentals recorded. These are growing in specialist collections or gardens.

The Species Accounts

Very few of Fiji's palms have English names or widely recognised Fijian names, so the species are identified throughout this book using their scientific names, which are always written in italics (for example, *Pritchardia pacifica* – one of the few palms which has an English name, Fiji fan palm). A scientific name consists of two words, the first being the name of the genus, which is a taxonomic group of closely related species. The second is the species name which represents a group of plants all possessing a common set of characteristics that sets them apart from another species.

Arrangement: The species accounts are separated into three sections: indigenous species, ancient introductions, and recent introductions. This is an artificial arrangement but is likely to be more convenient for non-specialists and emphasises the difference between indigenous and introduced but naturalised species.

Heading: Each species is identified by its botanical name and an explanation of the meaning or derivation of this scientific name. If available, the common English name is given here. Fijian names are not given here but they are included in the Cultural Use section because there are often several names that require explanation for any one species.

Description: As far as is practical, the description of the palm is given in non-technical language. A glossary at the end of the book assists with 'botanical' terms. The description focuses on readily visible characteristics and does not delve into important characteristics of the flowers and seeds which are used in the positive identification of some species. This may be irritating for the specialist, but to describe these palms in greater detail is beyond the scope and intention of this book.

With the recent re-classification of the *Veitchia* reducing the number of species from nine to five, much of the difficulty of identification in this group has been removed, and with one exception, Taveuni, where both *V. filifera* and *V. simulans* occur, the medium-sized *Veitchia* are identifiable by island location. *V. joannis* does occur with each of the other *Veitchia* but is much larger and readily identifiable. However, *V. filifera* and *V. vitiensis* both show a great deal of variation in some of the most readily observable characteristics (height, trunk diameter, number of leaves, crownshaft colouring etc), so new observers should be wary of this.

The most difficult to identify are the *Balaka* and it is probable that when these are given some serious study, there will be changes to the current taxonomy as well as new species described.

Distribution: The distribution of the species is given as far as it is known. It must be realised that while we have a good knowledge of the inter-island distribution of our palms (though we continue to be surprised, for instance the recent finding of *Hydriastele vitiensis* on Vanua Levu), the intra-island distribution is poorly known for many species. The island(s) on which a palm occurs is mentioned, as well as the areas, usually by describing provinces or mountains.

Habitat and Ecology: This section provides an overview of the ecological requirements of the palm, usually reflecting different forest types, height above sea level or rainfall requirements.

Cultural Uses: In this section what is known about Fijian uses and the various names of the palm are described.

For Fijian names, Standard Fijian spelling is used which has the following conventions:

g is pronounced **ng** (as in singer);

q is pronounced **ngg** (as in finger);

c is pronounced **th** (as in that);

b is pronounced **mb** (as in number) and

d is pronounced **nd** (as in tender).

Conservation: The conservation significance and the threat status of the species is described with some discussion on the threats themselves and current trends (see section 'Conservation Threat Status of Fiji's Palms' on page 40, for an explanation of the criteria used).

Illustrations

George Bennett has magnificently illustrated all 25 of Fiji's native palms, as well as five of the naturalised species. Fruit of all but three of the native palms are also illustrated. Each of the illustrations is from a growing palm, nearly all of them in the wild. The illustration captions indicate where the palms were found.

Distribution Maps

The distribution maps have been prepared to show where the palms are currently known to occur. The maps show the relief of Fiji with forest cover draped over it. The forest cover is slightly modified from the real situation – see the forest cover maps in the next section. In these distribution maps, forest blocks are consolidated, judged to be those which appear to have a chance of long-term survival. Mahogany plantations are blocked in brown.

Dylan Fuller (1997) has prepared distribution maps for most Fijian palms based on authenticated records. The maps here extend these to all species and in addition, records based on my own identifications and others that I have gleaned from knowledgeable people. The majority of these are very likely to be correct but they are not authenticated by specimens.

Access to Wild Growing Palms

Those wanting to see palms in the wild must first appreciate that almost all the palms are growing on land owned by Fijian communities and they must get permission from the owners before entering the land. Finding the owners is not always an easy or straightforward exercise. It is usually best not to ask the first Fijian you see but to go to the closest village and ask to speak to the village headman, the *turaganikoro*, who will be able to advise you on who the owners are and what procedures are required.

Fiji: the Country, Vegetation and the Palm Flora

The Fiji Islands

Fiji (officially The Republic of the Fiji Islands) is an archipelago located between 16-20°S, 177°W and 175°E. There are four major islands in the group: Viti Levu, Vanua Levu, Taveuni and Kadavu. Of the more than 320 islands, approximately 100 are inhabited.

The Fiji archipelago is positioned on a distinct, triangular tectonic plate with a complicated and perhaps not fully understood tectonic history. Geologically, the islands, with a few exceptions, comprise mainly late Eocene to Recent volcanic and volcaniclastic rocks. The oldest dated rocks are in the range 40 to 36 million years, while the most recent volcanic eruptions that have been dated occurred approximately 2000 years ago on Taveuni. Some maintain that Taveuni is still volcanically active. Other types of islands include raised-limestone islands (makatea) and a few true atolls. Some areas of Viti Levu and the Lau Group have karst (limestone) features and soils.

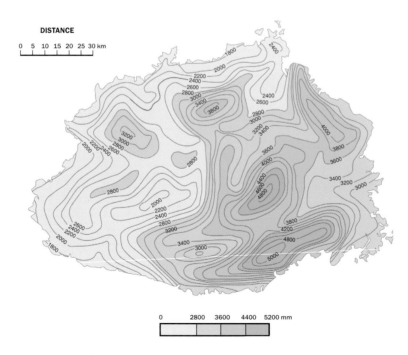

Rainfall distribution for the island of Viti Levu (isohyetal map).

Topographically, the volcanic islands are mainly steep and rugged. The highest mountain is Tomaniivi at 1323 metres.

Biological evidence, not as yet supported by geological evidence, increasingly suggests that Fiji has at some point had a direct continental connection, either through the presence of a continental terrane (or an offshore island of an ancient landmass) buried under volcanics or eroded away or submerged, or through a direct encounter with a Gondwana terrane such as 'Eua (in Tonga) that has subsequently moved away.

Fiji's climate is tropical oceanic and dominated by the southeast trade winds. Mean monthly temperatures range from 23°C in July to 28°C in January. Topography has a large effect on rainfall distribution as shown by the isohyetal maps below. Windward sides of the larger islands receive 1200-6000 mm of rainfall annually, with some coastal peaks receiving over 10,000 mm while low-lying coastal strips on the leeward sides receive less than 1200 mm annually. In areas on the leeward sides of the larger islands, a dry season frequently lasts from May to October when drought conditions can occur. The wet season over the whole group is from November to April, when cyclones are more likely to occur.

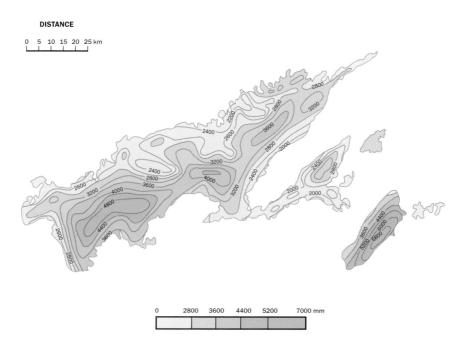

Rainfall distribution for the islands of Vanua Levu and Tavenui (isohyetal map).

Fiji's Flora & Vegetation

Introduction

Fiji's flora is well known by comparison with many Pacific Island states and A.C. Smith's six-volume *Flora Vitiensis Nova* is an unparalleled resource. Over half (56 percent) of Fiji's 1594 indigenous plant species are archipelagic endemics, and many display very limited ranges within Fiji. Several Fijian plant taxa, such as palms (25 spp., 96 percent endemism), *Psychotria* (76 spp., 95 percent endemic) and *Cyrtandra* (37 spp., 100 percent endemic) have developed an almost entirely endemic complement of species. Of the 476 plant genera native to Fiji, 90 percent are shared with New Guinea, and 65 percent to 75 percent of these are also found in northern Australia, New Caledonia, and other islands of Western Melanesia. The remaining 10 percent of Fijian plant genera are either endemic or restricted to the Pacific. Within habitats, the greatest

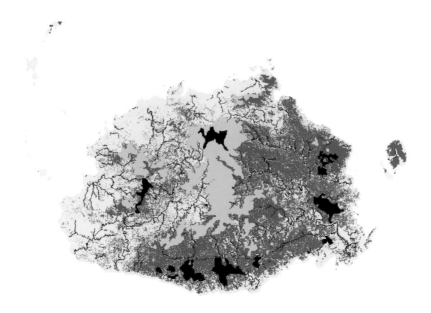

ISLAND OF VITI LEVU
Green: Forest remaining on Viti Levu
Pale Green: Forest over 800 metres
Black: Hardwood Plantations
(Original Source: 1994 Fiji Natural Forest Inventory).

concentration of endemic plants and invertebrates occurs within moist forests, with especially high percentages within the moss or cloud forests on the highest peaks. The plant family Degeneriaceae, with its two species, is endemic to Fiji.

Prior to human arrival, Fiji was covered in closed-canopy forest but today only about 45 percent of Fiji's main islands remain forested, with varying degrees of degradation. Forest fragmentation and deforestation are ongoing and there are relatively few solid forest blocks remaining, as can be seen from the figures below.

Rainforest Vegetation

Lowland Rainforest

The characteristic forest type of the wet zone of the larger islands, extending from near sea level to an altitude of 600m and receiving a mean annual rainfall range of 2000-3000 mm. The tallest stands of forest trees are found in such forest and may grow up to 30m in height. Common dominant tree species include: *Calophyllum vitiense*, **Damanu**; *Palaquium hornei*, **Sacau**; *Myristica*

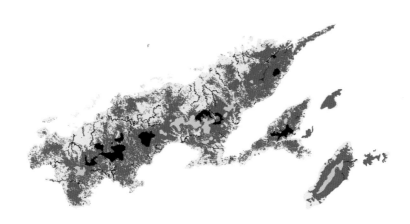

ISLANDS OF VANUA LEVU AND TAVEUNI
Green: Forest remaining on Vanua Levu
Pale Green: Forest over 800 metres
Black: Hardwood Plantations
(Original Source: 1994 Fiji Natural Forest Inventory).

spp., **Kaudamu**; *Endiandra gillespiei*, **Damabi**; *Agathis macrophyllum*, **Dakua makadre**; *Parinari insularis*, **Sa**; *Syzygium* spp., **Yasiyasi**; *Cleistocalyx* spp., **Yasiyasi**; *Endospermum macrophyllum*, **Kauvula**; *Trichospermum* spp., **Mako**; *Canarium vitiense*, **Kaunicina**; *Barringtonia edulis*, **Vutu kana**; *Heritiera ornithocephala*, **Rosarosa**; *Garcinia* spp., **Laubu**; *Alphitonia* spp., **Doi**. Species composition in this forest type varies according to aspect, soil and location.

Upland Rainforest

Such forest type occurs mostly in areas above 600m in the wet and dry zones, the latter towards the interior of the large islands. The areas receive a mean annual rainfall range of 2000-4000 mm. On Viti Levu it includes the Nadrau Plateau and its surrounding mountain ranges, Rairaimatuku Plateau and the Korobasabasaga range in the wet zone; and in the dry zone the Mt Evans-Koroyanitu range, Naloto range and Nausori Highlands. Conifers often dominate this forest type. Dominant tree species found here include those species found in the lowland rainforest: *Agathis macrophyllum*, **Dakua madadre**; *Dysoxylum richii*, **Sasawira**; *Dacrydium nidulum*, **Yaka** and especially *Metrosideros* spp. **Vuga** and *Podocarpus neriifolius*, **Kuasi**. More common subcanopy trees include *Alstonia montana*, **Drega**; *Glochidion* spp. **Molau**; and *Mussaenda raiateensis*, **Bovu**.

Montane Forest

This forest type has generally abundant epiphytes and is dominated by angiosperms and starts at about 800m. *Metrosideros collina*, **Vuda** species of *Syzygium*, various species in the Rubiaceae and palms are commonly part of this vegetation type.

Cloud Forest

Cloud forest occupies about 50-100 square kilometres scattered above 600-900m on the ridges and peaks of Fiji's largest islands. On Mt Koroturaga in Taveuni a mean annual rainfall of 9970 mm over five years was recorded. The trees are stunted with their trunks covered with mosses and a relatively thick litter layer covered with mosses on the substrate surface. This extremely dense forest has a canopy of about 7m and is dominated by tree ferns (*Cyathea* spp. **Balabala**, *Dicksonia brackenridgei*), *Dysoxylum gillespieanum*, **Maletawa**; *Hernandia moerenhoutiana*; *Clinostigma exorrhizum*, **Niuniu**; *Weinmannia* spp.; *Syzygium* spp., **Yasiyasi**; *Macaranga seemannii*, **Mama**; *Podocarpus affinis*, **Kuasi**; *Paphia vitiensis*, **Vuga**; and *Leptopteris* ferns with an abundance of climbing *Freycinetia* spp. The abundance of epiphytic orchids and cryptophytes, filmy ferns, tree ferns, species of *Weinmannia* and *Paphia vitiensis* are characteristic of this forest type in Fiji.

Dry Forest

Evergreen Dry Forest

In the drier zones, seasonal or dry forest once occurred extensively. Today such forest types occur to any extent only in parts of the dry zone of Vanua Levu having a mean annual rainfall range of 1000-2250 mm. Fijian dry forests are on the wetter end of the spectrum for dry forests and thus they are not particularly deciduous. Nearly all Fiji's dry forests have been converted to agriculture, scrubs of introduced plants or talasiga grasslands.

Transition forests occur between the wet and dry zones, roughly along a SW-NE belt on the larger islands and at mid-elevations on taller ranges within the dry zone. This forest is generally dominated by tree *Dacrydium nidulum*, **Yaka**; *Fagraea gracilipes*, **Buabua** and *Gymnostoma vitiense*, **Velau**. Other common or characteristic trees may include *Podocarpus neriifolius*, **Kuasi**; *Myristica castaneifolia*, **Yasiyasi**; *Dysoxylum richii*, **Sasawira**; *Cycas seemannii*, **Logologo**; *Parinari insularum*, **Sa**; *Intsia bijuga*, **Vesi**; species of *Syzygium Yasiyasi* and members of the Sapotaceae and Rubiaceae. Formerly, *Santalum yasi,* **Yasi** may have been a characteristic member of this forest type.

Deciduous Coastal Dry Forest

Recent studies have revealed a forest type that has several deciduous canopy species. *Gyrocarpus americanus*, **Wiriwiri** is the most common and the most characteristic of these. Other common deciduous species include *Pongamia pinnata*, **Vesiwai**; *Pleiogynium timoriense*, **Manui**; *Garuga floribunda*, **Yamo**; *Koelreuteria elegans*, **Manawi** and a yet unknown species of the Sapindaceae, many of which are probably drought-deciduous. Nevertheless, evergreen species are usually more common and include taxa such as *Kingiodendron platycarpum*, **Moivi** and species of *Maniltoa*, **Moivi** as well as *Planchonella grayana*, **Bausa** and species of *Manilkara*, **Baubulu**. The most common understorey species are probably *Mallotus tiliifolius, Vavaea amicorum*, **Cevua** and species of *Diospyros*, **Kaukauloa**.

Coastal and Wetland Vegetation

Mangrove Forest

This is found along the coastline and is especially associated with river estuaries. The most common species are the two *Rhizophora*, **Tiri** species and their hybrid, and *Bruguiera gymnorrhiza*, **Dogo**. Other tree species include *Xylocarpus granatum*, **Dabi**; *Lumnitzera littorea*, **Sagali**; *Heritiera littoralis*, **Kedra ivi**; and *Excoecaria agallocha*, **Sinu gaga**.

Coastal Strand Vegetation

On Viti Levu, much of this vegetation has been removed by human activity; however, though it remains in some secluded areas, though rarely as dense as found on some of the smaller and uninhabited islands. Strand vegetation generally displays a distinct zonation, with creepers and herbs at the seaward edge merging with hardy shrubs, before giving way to trees. The more common plants include the creepers *Ipomoea pes-caprae*, **Lawere**; *Vigna marina*, **Drautolu** and the grasses *Lepturus repens*, **Vutika** and *Sporobolus* spp.

The shrubs mainly comprise of *Scaevola taccada*, **Vivevedu**; *Sophora tomentosa*, *Vitex trifolia*, **Dralakaka** and trees include *Calophyllum inophyllum*, **Dilo**; *Intsia bijuga*, **Vesi**; *Acacia simplicifolia*, **Tatagia**; *Terminalia litoralis*, **Tavola damu**; *Hibiscus tiliaceus*, **Vau**, and *Pandanus tectorius*, **Vadra**.

Freshwater Wetland Vegetation

Such vegetation type occurs on Viti Levu's wet zone in poorly drained alluvial sites along coastal flats, some of which are quite large peat swamps, and limited areas along the Rewa and Navua rivers. The flora of Viti Levu's wetlands is very heavily influenced by introduced weedy species. Common species include the sedges *Eleocharis* spp., **Kuta** and *Cyperus haspan*, the ferns *Dicranopteris* spp., **Qato**; *Nephrolepsis biserrata* and *Lycopodium cernuum*, the grass *Brachiara mutica* and the trees *Annona glabra*, **Utonibulumakau**; *Barringtonia racemosa*, **Vutuwai**; *Inocarpus fagifer*, **Ivi**; *Hibiscus tiliaceus*, **Vau**, and *Pandanus* spp. **Vadra** are common.

There also freshwater lakes and associated wetlands on the Udu Peninsula in Vanua Levu and the Tagimoucia Crater Lake on Taveuni that are more pristine.

River Vegetation

Although there is no extensive river vegetation because rivers are too small, there are certain plants that are restricted to growing on the banks of rivers, where they are inundated during swells after the frequent rains. These 'river specialists' include several ferns, *Syzygium seemannianum*, **Yasiwai**; *Ficus bambusifolia*, **Loseloseniwai**; *Acalypha rivularis*, **Kadakada**; and other species.

Disturbed Vegetation

Talasiga Grasslands

This dry zone vegetation is found in fire-degraded environments and spreads from sea level to 1000m and receives a mean annual rainfall range of 1500-2500 mm. The vegetation is mainly composed of the shrubby ferns *Dicranopteris linearis*, **Qato** and *Pteridium esculentum*, **Qato** the grasses *Sporobolus indicus* and *Pennisetum polystachyon* and the reed *Miscanthus floridulus*, **Gasau**. The more common shrubs include *Pandanus* spp., **Vadra**; *Leucaena leucocephala*, **Vaivai**; *Dodonea viscosa*, **Wase**; *Alstonia montana*, **Drega**; *Grewia crenata*, **Siti**; *Morinda citrifolia*, **Kura**; and *Mussaenda raiateensis*, **Bovu**.

The trees include *Mangifera indica*, **Maqo**; *Casuarina equisitifiolia*, **Nokonoko** and *Albizia lebbeck*, **Vaivai** with *Paraserianthes saman*, **Vaivai** dominating gulley and creek vegetation.

Secondary Forest

Forests that are recovering from logging or other catastrophic events have a high proportion of early successional species such as species of *Alphitonia*, **Doi**; *Macaranga*, **Davo**; *Dendrocnide harveyi*, **Salato**, and *Trichospermum*, **Mako**. The invasive African Tulip Tree, *Spathodea campanulata*, **Pisipisi** is beginning to dominate many of these forests.

Fiji's Palm Flora

Overview

By comparison with some other botanical groups, Fiji's palm flora is well researched, but there is much yet to learn. A brief summary of changes in our 'palm flora' over the dozen years to 2005 shows how rapidly changes are occurring:

- Three new species described – *Heterospathe phillipsii, Balaka streptostachys* and *Hydriastele boumae;*
- There are at least two taxa awaiting scientific description, almost certainly new species – *Balaka* 'bulitavu' and *Cyphosperma* 'naboutini'.
- Our *Veitchia* species have been comprehensively revised – reduced from nine species to four; and,
- *Goniocladus petiolatus* (a 'lost' palm) has been found to be *Physokentia rosea*.

There are many forest areas in Fiji that remain to be properly surveyed for palms. Just when we feel a certain comfort as to what to expect and where, our complacency gets shaken. So it was when Timoci Bulitavu showed Dr Will McLatchey a small population of *Clinostigma exorrhizum* surviving very nicely at sea level, way up in the north of Vanua Levu; everywhere else this palm is definitely a high altitude or cloud forest species.

There are surely plenty more surprises in store for palm enthusiasts wishing to put a bit of effort in. At present, however, Fiji's palm flora is recognised to consist of 31 species in 16 genera, of which 25 are indigenous and 6 are naturalised introductions. Of the 25 indigenous species all but one, *Calamus vitiensis*, and perhaps *Pritchardia pacifica*, are endemic. There is some debate as to whether the latter is indeed native to Fiji, but we believe it to be so on linguistic grounds, its presence in mature forest on the Rotuman island of Uea and the strong possibility that the *Pritchardia* palms evolved in this part of the Pacific. If it is not indigenous, it is certainly a very early introduction and of long cultural significance to Fijians.

Of the naturalised species, the ubiquitous coconut may or may not be a human-assisted introduction, but the other five surely are. The coconut and *Metroxylon warburgii* are of ancient introduction, the remaining four more recent, with the latest, *Pinanga coronata*, an unwanted invasive species which arrived in the 1970s at Coloisuva and is now spreading aggressively.

Relationships

Fiji's flora, as a whole, has very strong floristic links with Melanesia and Southeast Asia. Around 90 percent of seed plant genera occur in New Guinea with about 70 percent in Australia, New Caledonia and intervening archipelagoes. Fiji's palm flora, however, shares its closest relationship at the generic level with Vanuatu (60 percent) which is well above its affinity with Solomon Islands (27 percent), Bismarck Archipelago (25 percent) and Samoa (15 percent). Fiji shares a single genus, *Cyphosperma*, with New Caledonia and also shares one, *Pritchardia*, with Hawaii and French Polynesia. Of interest too, is how many palm genera reach Fiji but go no further into the Pacific. For eight (75 percent) of Fiji's indigenous palm genera, *(Alsmithia, Calamus, Cyphosperma, Heterospathe, Hydriastele, Metroxylon, Neoveitchia* and *Physokentia)*, Fiji is the southern or eastern limit. This reflects the position Fiji holds in being the easternmost outpost in Oceania of a diverse, moist tropical rainforest.

Diversity and Distribution

Depending on whether *Pritchardia pacifica* is regarded as indigenous or not, Fiji's palms exhibit a remarkable 92 percent or 96 percent endemism at the specific level. However, with the recent discovery[1] of a *Neoveitchia* in Vanuatu, only one of Fiji's 16 indigenous palm genera, *Alsmithia*, is endemic at the generic level. This appears to indicate relatively recent, long distance colonisation of source material. Whether this is mainly from Vanuatu (reflecting the 60 percent shared genera) or whether both received source material independently from the Solomons-Papua New Guinea region, requires further study. Within Fiji, speciation of this source material has presumably been relatively rapid and primarily of an inter-island rather than intra-island nature with 10 (40 percent) of the palms restricted to a single island, indicating that dispersal between islands is rather difficult. Interestingly, only one species – the normally 'highland' *Clinostigma exorrhizum* – is found naturally on four or more islands.[2] *Veitchia joannis* has the most extensive range in the wild of our palms, but humans are almost certainly primarily responsible for this. Currently the three largest islands share a similar number of those palms which are not widespread in the group: Viti Levu and Vanua Levu have 11 and Taveuni has 9. The species island pairs are somewhat surprising, not following any particular pattern:

• Viti Levu and Vanua Levu share two – *Balaka macrocarpa, Hydriastele vitiensis (Metroxylon*

[1] Dowe, J.L. and P. Cabalion. 1996. A taxonomic account of Arecaceae in Vanuatu, with descriptions of three new species. *Aust. Syst. Bot.* 9:1-60.
[2] In respect of *Veitchia vitiensis* – Ovalau as a 'land-bridge' island is considered part of Viti Levu.

vitiense is considered introduced to Vanua Levu);

- Vanua Levu and Taveuni share five – *Alsmithia longipes, Balaka seemannii, Cyphosperma trichospadix, Physokentia thurstonii* and *Veitchia filifera.*
- Viti Levu and Taveuni share one – *Calamus vitiensis.*
- Viti Levu and Gau also share one – *Physokentia petiolatus.*

Altitude is often a distribution determinant amongst plants and this is true of Fiji's palms; however, it is rarely altitude *per se* but associated characteristics such as high rainfall, high frequency of cloud cover and low frequency or absence of drought conditions. This is the case with Fiji's palms; certain species are clearly 'highland' in character – *Clinostigma exorrhizum,*[3] *Cyphosperma tanga, Cyphosperma trichospadix* and *Hydriastele boumae* are the most extreme, with *Physokentia petiolatus* and *Hydriastele vitiensis* fairly close behind. However, in certain places where conditions are right, these species are found at much lower altitude than usual; for instance *Hydriastele boumae* is found down at less than 100m in the Bouma area of northwest Taveuni, possibly the wettest lowland area in Fiji. On Viti Levu *Physokentia petiolatus* and *Clinostigma exorrhizum* are most common at higher altitudes around Nadarivatu, Tomaniivi and the Rairaimatuku Plateau, but they are both found at much lower altitudes on the exposed ridges of southern Viti Levu's coastal mountain chain, as well as on Gau Island where ridges as low as 300m intercept the southeast trade winds and provide a buffered 'wet' climate.

Much more difficult to explain are the extremely restricted ranges of many of Fiji's palms. Indeed, 12 (48 percent) of our indigenous palms have restricted or very restricted ranges (refer to Table 1).

One can but wonder whether insect pests fuelled by the extensive coconut plantations of the copra industry may have had something to do with it. It is interesting to note that Fiji's Copra Industry owes its very survival to the biological control of not one pest but at least five. One of these was so successful that the pest, the attractive Levuana moth, is almost certainly now extinct.[4] This is well known, but what is not known is whether these pests were able to cross over and attack native palms. We know at least one of these did, the rhinoceros beetle on *Neoveitchia storckii* and in certain cases *Veitchia joannis* but there may well have been others and more seriously. There is circumstantial evidence that the status of *N. storckii* has improved since the control of the rhinoceros beetle following the introduction of a virus in the mid-1970s. If this is the case, then

---

[3] Though the finding of a population of *Clinostigma exorrhizum* near sea level at Wainika, Vanua Levu is strange and warrants further research.

[4] For more on this subject see the chapter 'Coconut Trilogy' in *Mai Veikau – Tales of Fijian Wildlife* by Dick Watling.

Table 1: Fiji Palms with Restricted Ranges

Species	Number of Separate Populations	Area of Occupancy
Balaka streptostachys	One	Less than 1 km^2
Balaka 'bulitavu'	One	Less than 1 km^2
Cyphosperma tanga	One remaining	Less than 4 km^2
Cyphosperma 'naboutini'	One	Less than 6 km^2
Balaka macrocarpa	Three – one on Viti Levu and two on Vanua Levu (but these may not all be the same taxa)	Less than 10 km^2
Balaka microcarpa	One	Less than 10 km^2
Heterospathe phillipsii	Two	Less than 10 km^2
Pritchardia thurstonii	Many different islets in three island groups	Less than 10 km^2
Cyphosperma trichospadix	At least three populations on Vanua Levu and Taveuni, but distribution very poorly known	Less than 4 km^2
Hydriastele vitiensis	At least three on Viti Levu's southern mountain chain and three in Vanua Levu	Less than 40 km^2
Hydriastele boumae	Probably single population in Taveuni's wettest forests	Less than 40 km^2
Neoveitchia storckii	A single dispersed population in central-eastern Viti Levu	Less than 60 km^2

perhaps some of the restricted range species are actually in a 'recovery' phase now.

Given the number of potential bird and bat dispersal agents for Fiji's palms, it is certainly surprising that there are any limited distribution species, on the large islands anyway. The role of rats as seed predators requires urgent clarification. All three species currently extant in the islands have been introduced since human colonisation. The Polynesian rat has been here for over 3000 years while the black and Norway rats about 175 years. Is this long enough for their seed predation to have become stabilised – in balance? The answer to that is no. Even the potential impact of the Polynesian rat could at very low levels of predation be a significant extra evolutionary pressure weighing against the survival of one or more palm species.

Now that the Polynesian rat has been largely usurped in the forests of the larger islands by the equally arboreal but larger ship rat, the pressure could be accentuated. We urgently need research on the community dynamics of our threatened palms, and the agents responsible for limiting seed production, distribution and germination.

Dispersal

The restricted ranges of many of our palms and the apparently large areas of forest which could be stocked with at least some of them, appears to indicate that dispersion and/or germination and establishment is a problem. Most palm specialists have concluded that dispersion is by water and gravity or by birds and bats, but there are very few recorded observations of this for native palms. In contrast, jungle mynahs *Acridotheres tristis* and red-vented bulbuls *Pycnonotus cafer* (neither bird is native to Fiji) are commonly seen feeding on the fruit of the naturalised *Ptychosperma macarthurii*[5] and *Pinanga coronata*, but neither of these birds inhabits native forest to any significant degree (they also feed on *Veitchia vitiensis* when these are grown in a suburban garden).

Julian Ash in his detailed study of *Balaka microcarpa*, a species with one of the most restricted ranges, found that each fruiting stalk produced on average 187 fruit to maturity. He concluded that about 5 percent of maturing fruits were obviously parasitised and that fallen fruit were rapidly removed or destroyed, though there were often a few seedlings within 2-3m of the base of flowering palms. He recorded no observations of fruits being eaten by birds or bats.

In the botanical literature, the only bird recorded feeding on fruit of Fiji's native palms appears to be the large masked shining parrot *Prosopeia personata*. The author, an ornithologist by inclination, has had a special interest in seed dispersal by Fijian birds and bats but has made only

---

[5] This is despite the reported very heavy concentration of irritant calcium oxalate in these seeds.

a few observations of birds feeding on native palm fruit. Table 2 (overleaf) provides a summary of observations, species and dispersal potential. It is clear from this table that there are plenty of potential dispersers of palm seeds, but we do not know the answers to some of the critical questions – do the seeds remain viable if they are ingested, and to what degree do these birds or bats actually feed on the fruit? Certainly a good research topic for an enterprising student.

It is important to make a distinction between seed dispersers and seed predators. For instance, the shining parrots *Prosopeia* spp. are seed predators, destroying the seed and extracting the endosperm. The shining parrots may carry large seeds *(Metroxylon, Alsmithia, Neoveitchia, Veitchia joannis)* and occasionally drop them before feeding but their primary purpose is to destroy them. In captivity, shining parrots easily penetrate and destroy tough seeds such as *Alsmithia, Neoveitchia* and *Veitchia joannis*. In the field, mass predation of nearly mature but still green *Balaka macrocarpa* fruit has been observed on several occasions, almost certainly caused by shining parrots, although rats cannot be completely ruled out. All Fiji's palm specialists have noted the difficulty in obtaining mature fruit of several species of palm, especially *Cyphosperma* spp. and *Balaka macrocarpa*.

Rats are not native to Fiji and are certainly predators of palm fruit, and also germinating seed.[6] Three species have been introduced: the Polynesian rat *Rattus exulans*, the ship rat *R. rattus* and the Norway rat. *R. exulans* arrived with Fiji's first human colonists,[7] *R. norvegicus* arrived with the first Europeans, and all three have readily become naturalised. On the large islands, it is the highly arboreal ship rat which is now the common rat in Fiji's forests, and its predation on seeds – *in situ*, fallen or germinating, could be a significant factor on the recruitment of native palms.

In the author's garden, rats feed on the fallen fruit of *V. joannis* and *N. storckii* and leave characteristic sign – they penetrate at the point of attachment with the seed stalk, gnaw straight into the endosperm (effectively ignoring the fleshy mesocarp) to obtain the embryo, and when this is extracted, they usually leave the fruit, although sometimes they eat a bit more of the endosperm.

However, it is the small island-inhabiting fan palm *Pritchardia thurstonii*, where the impact of rat predation is possibly seen most clearly, though this remains hypothetical for the time being. These palms survive only on small lagoonal, limestone islands in the Vulaga and Ogea group and the Sovu islets of Vanuabalavu. There are many hundreds of hectares of similar karst limestone habitat on the 'main islands' and adjacent more fertile alkaline soils under forest, but the palm is

[6] Rats have on several occasions 'invaded' the author's nursery and dug up and eaten newly planted-out seedlings. On one occasion, these were trapped and proved to be the ship rat.
[7] Currently dated at approximately 3300 years ago based on a recently found Lapita site at Rove in southwest Viti Levu.

Table 2: Potential Dispersers of Palm Seeds in Fiji's Forests

Disperser	Species	Distribution	Observations & Dispersal Characteristics
BIRDS			
Jungle fowl	*Gallus gallus*	Introduced and now remains on Taveuni and a few other islands without the mongoose	Potential disperser of fallen fruit; more of a forest edge species at lower altitudes
White-throated pigeon	*Columba vitiensis*	Larger islands only	Not a true frugivore, but a potential disperser of smaller palm fruit; has a gizzard and so seeds may not be viable
Friendly ground dove	*Gallicolumba stairii*	Low density on large islands, common on some smaller islands	Potential disperser of small and, perhaps, medium-sized palm fruit seeds
Pacific pigeon	*Ducula pacifica*	Absent from the larger islands	True frugivore, but does not occur on the larger islands where most palms are found
Barking pigeon	*Ducula latrans*	Larger and medium-sized islands	True frugivore; has been observed feeding on *V. joannis, V. vitiensis, Hydriastele boumae*. Common and a good potential disperser of all medium and large palm fruit.
Many-coloured fruit dove	*Ptilinopus perousii*	Larger islands only	Fig specialist but might take small and medium-sized palm fruit opportunistically
Crimson-crowned fruit dove	*Ptilinopus porphyraceus*	Absent from the larger islands	True frugivore, but does not occur on the larger islands where most palms are found
Golden dove	*Ptilinopus luteovirens*	Viti Levu, Gau	Specialist forest understorey fruit eaters and good potential dispersers of palm seeds. Observed feeding on *V. vitiensis*
Orange dove	*Ptilinopus victor*	Vanua Levu, Taveuni	Specialist forest understorey fruit eaters and good potential dispersers of palm seeds. Observed feeding on *V. filifera*
Whistling dove	*Ptilinopus layardi*	Kadavu	Specialist forest understorey fruit eaters and good potential dispersers of palm seeds
Masked shining parrot	*Prosopeia personata*	Viti Levu and formerly Ovalau	Seed predator – only likely to disperse occasionally large palm fruit – *Metroxylon, Neoveitchia, V. joannis* etc.
Red shining parrot	*Prosopeia tabuensis*	Vanua Levu, Taveuni, Koro, Gau	Seed predator – occasional disperser of large palm seeds, *Alsmithia, V. joannis*. Captive birds readily feed on any palm seed presented, irrespective of size.

Disperser	Species	Distribution	Observations & Dispersal Characteristics
BIRDS			
Kadavu shining parrot	*Prosopeia splendens*	Kadavu	Seed predator – occasional disperser of large palm seeds – *V. joannis*
Polynesian triller	*Lalage maculosa*	Widespread	In forest, tends to be a canopy-only species – potential disperser of small palm fruit – *Clinostigma, Heterospathe, Hydriastele vitiensis*
Red-vented bulbul	*Pycnonotus cafer*	Larger islands only	A good small-seed disperser but does not go into the forest where most palms are. Observed feeding on the fruit of *Veitchia vitiensis*
Island thrush	*Turdus poliocephalus*	Larger islands only	A good small and medium-sized seed disperser; has been observed feeding on fruit of *Physokentia petiolatus*
Fiji white-eye	*Zosterops explorator*	Larger islands only	A potential disperser of small palm fruit – *Heterospathe, Clinostigma, Hydriastele vitiensis*
Silvereye	*Zosterops lateralis*	Widespread	A forest edge species, will not come into contact with native palms
Polynesian starling	*Aplonis tabuensis*	Widespread	A good small and medium-sized seed disperser; has been observed feeding on fruit of *Hydriastele boumae*
Jungle mynah	*Acridotheres fuscus*	Larger islands only	Major disperser of *Ptychosperma macarthurii* but does not enter forest. Feeds on *Veitchia vitiensis* in garden situations
FRUIT BATS			
Pacific flying fox	*Pteropus tonganus*	Very widespread	A potential disperser of large fruit *Alsmithia, Neoveitchia, Veitchia joannis* and even *V. filifera, V. vitiensis* and *V. simulans*. Has been observed feeding on *V. joannis, V. filifera* and *Neoveitchia*
Samoan flying fox	*Pteropus samoensis*	Larger islands only	A potential disperser of large and medium-sized palm fruit
Fiji flying fox	*Pteralopex acrodonta*	Endemic to Taveuni	A potential disperser of large and medium-sized palm fruit
Pacific blossom bat	*Notopteris macdonaldii*	Viti Levu, Vanua Levu, Taveuni	As far as is known, a nectivorous and pollen feeder, not a fruit eater or potential palm seed disperser

not found naturally here today, although they survive well when transplanted. Absence of seed-eating rats (or some other predator) on the islets would seem to be the most likely explanation.

The evolutionary impact of rats does not have to be immediate and final, continuous low-level seed predation on a poorly dispersing palm or tree species may be sufficient to gradually tip the balance towards range contraction and extinction. This may take hundreds or even thousands of years.

Flying foxes habitually carry seeds to favoured eating spots and, in contrast to shining parrots, they are excellent dispersers of seeds, because they are primarily 'fruit pulp processors', spitting out intact seeds and wads of fibre after their large molars have crushed out the juice and pulp. The Pacific flying fox *Pteropus tonganus* has been observed feeding on and dropping *Veitchia joannis* and *V. filifera* fruit, while *Neoveitchia* fruit with flying fox teethmarks have also been observed. Of great interest is the fragrance of ripe *Alsmithia longipes* fruit. The only purpose of this would seem to be to attract flying foxes for dispersal purposes.

In the last few years, it has been discovered that prior to the arrival of humans, Fiji had a remarkable 'megafauna'. This consisted of at least three megapodes including a giant flightless form, a dodo-sized flightless pigeon, at least one other large pigeon, a giant iguana, a tortoise, a giant frog and a terrestrial crocodile. With the exception of the last two, all may have been involved in the dispersal of fruit seeds including palms. However, their current absence would be unlikely to impact palm fruit dispersal, given the existence of apparently suitable alternative and more appropriately-sized frugivorous birds and bats.

It is surprising that with so many potential bird and bat dispersers for Fiji's palms, so many of them have very restricted ranges. While rats are clearly a serious predator of palm seed, but by no means yet proven as limiting any species' regeneration, there may be other less conspicuous predators and the role of insects clearly needs close examination.

Conservation

The Forests and Forestry

Fiji retains about 45-50 percent forest cover and it is here where all Fiji's palms are found with the partial exception of *Metroxylon vitiense*. Much of this forest has been selectively logged or is affected by fire; consequently, only 20 percent of the forest remaining is 'dense' forest. Yet most if not all of Fiji's palms survive well in logged-over forest.

Although there is forestry legislation and a Code of Logging Practice, most of the logging causes unacceptably high damage. The lack of any Environmental Impact Assessment or consideration of biodiversity values such as rare and threatened palms (or other species) prior to logging licenses being issued, directly threatens those palms with extremely small populations, and this is not acceptable by any standards in the 21st century.

However, the most significant forest conservation issue in the past 40 years has not been logging or deforestation but the conversion of about 50,000 hectares of good tropical rainforest to mahogany plantation and with it the loss of its bird and biodiversity values. This area had the potential to remain as sustainably-harvested tropical rainforest, retaining most of its biodiversity values. The conversion is particularly unfortunate because it was assisted for many years by foreign aid donors (Australia and New Zealand) and it ignored the very large areas of degraded forest where mahogany plantations could and should have been established without major implications for biodiversity.

Five of Fiji's most endangered palms have been or may be greatly impacted by mahogany plantations – *Balaka microcarpa*, *B. macrocarpa*, *Hydriastele vitiensis*, *Cyphosperma tanga* and *C.* 'naboutini', while *B. streptostachys* and *B.* 'bulitavu' are both in a prospective mahogany planting area. The mahogany plantations are currently coming online for harvesting and will soon support a major industry. It can only be hoped that this does not stimulate further rainforest conversion and that the Fiji Government realises that such conversion is a short-sighted and unsustainable practice. We need to encourage the mahogany industry in Fiji to become 'certified' as coming from sustainably managed plantations. This will improve its market worth, prevent the further conversion of rainforest and ensure that the species impacted by the existing plantations are rigorously protected.

Table 3: Distribution, Threats and Threat Statuses for Fiji's Palms*

Botanical Name	Island Distribution in Fiji	Current Conservation Threats	Protected Area Occurrence	IUCN Global Conservation Status*
Alsmithia longipes	Taveuni, Vanua Levu	Small population	Ravilevu N.R.; Bouma Heritage Park, Taveuni Forest Reserve	Endangered (Vulnerable)
Balaka longirostris	Viti Levu	Logging	Tomaniivi Nature Reserve, Wabu Forest Reserve	Least concern
Balaka macrocarpa	Viti Levu, Vanua Levu	Small population, Logging, mahogany plantations		Critically endangered
Balaka microcarpa	Viti Levu	Small population, Logging, mahogany plantations	Coloisuva Forest Park	Endangered (Critically Endangered)
Balaka seemannii	Taveuni, Vanua Levu	Logging; forest clearance	Ravilevu N.R.; Bouma Heritage Park	Least concern
Balaka streptostachys	Vanua Levu	Logging, new mahogany plantation		Critically endangered
Balaka 'bulitavu'	Vanua Levu	Logging, new mahogany plantation		Data deficient (Critically endangered)
Calamus vitiensis	Taveuni, Viti Levu		Ravilevu N.R.; Bouma Heritage Park	Least concern
Clinostigma exorrhizum	Viti Levu, Vanua Levu, Taveuni, Gau		Ravilevu N.R.; Bouma Heritage Park; Taveuni Forest Reserve	Least concern
Cyphosperma tanga	Viti Levu	Very small population, logging, plantation, formerly		Critically endangered
Cyphosperma trichospadix	Taveuni, Vanua Levu	Logging	Taveuni Forest Reserve	Vulnerable
Cyphosperma 'naboutini'	Viti Levu	Very small population, Logging, mahogany plantations		Critically endangered
Heterospathe phillipsii	Viti Levu	Small population, Logging		Endangered

Where there are changes, the author's currently recommended threat statuses are given in brackets.

Botanical Name	Island Distribution in Fiji	Current Conservation Threats	Protected Area Occurrence	IUCN Global Conservation Status*
Hydriastele boumae	Taveuni		Ravilevu N.R.; Bouma Heritage Park; Taveuni Forest Reserve	Data deficient (Least Concern)
Hydriastele vitiensis	Viti Levu, Vanua Levu	Small population, logging, mahogany plantations		Vulnerable
Metroxylon vitiense	Viti Levu, Ovalau	Unrestricted exploitation for heart of palm and to a lesser extent house thatch		Vulnerable
Neoveitchia storckii	**Viti Levu**	**Small population, forest conversion for agriculture, mahogany**		**Endangered**
Physokentia petiolatus	Viti Levu, Gau		Tomaniivi Nature Reserve, Wabu Forest Reserve	Near Threatened
Physokentia thurstonii	Taveuni, Vanua Levu	Distribution poorly known	Ravilevu N.R.; Bouma Heritage Park; Taveuni Forest Reserve	Near Threatened
Pritchardia pacifica	Widespread			Not evaluated
Pritchardia thurstonii	Islets of Vulaga, Ogea and Vanuabalavu	Small and fragmented populations		Vulnerable
Veitchia filifera	Vanua Levu, Taveuni	Logging, mahogany plantations. Forest conversion for agriculture	Waisali Reserve	Least concern
Veitchia joannis	Widespread	Forest conversion for agriculture	Koroyanitu Heritage Park	Least concern
Veitchia simulans	Taveuni	Forest conversion for agriculture	Ravilevu N.R.; Bouma Heritage Park; Taveuni Forest Reserve	Vulnerable
Veitchia vitiensis	Viti Levu, Ovalau, Kadavu, Beqa	Logging, mahogany plantations. Forest conversion for agriculture	Garrick Memorial Park, Coloisuva F.R.	Least concern

Protected Areas

Fiji completely lacks a system of scientifically-selected Protected Areas and there is little prospect that it will achieve such a goal in the near future. While there are some nominal Protected Areas, none has been identified on the basis of their biodiversity or ecological values and all are passively managed. They remain confusing in terms of their establishment, authority and tenure, level of protection, legislation, and in many cases boundaries. However, there appears to be an emerging sense of responsibility and willingness to initiate management in some of these protected areas in at least three of the key players, the National Trust for Fiji, the Forestry Department and the Department of the Environment, but their resources are woefully inadequate. Much will depend on how they can harness the resources and energy of a variety of non-government organisations that are emerging as key conservation players in Fiji.

The vast majority of Fiji's forests are owned by local communities which have primary authority over their use. As such, government cannot easily decree protected areas. Enabling forest protection invariably depends on the provision of monetary compensation to landowners to replace potential logging income, or on providing viable alternative development opportunities. Obtaining the commitment of landowners to conservation areas and conservation-compatible resource use is the only approach for successful protected areas. In such cases long-term engagement of the landowners is essential and creative approaches to ensuring they benefit from conservation urgently need to be developed.

Only on Taveuni do current protected areas provide conservation for Fiji's palms, as elsewhere very few of the country's threatened palms occur in secure protected areas (refer Table 3). A priority protected area would be the foothills of Mt Sorolevu in Vanua Levu, for without doubt, here is the richest palm flora in Fiji, with nine species all within a few kilometers of one another. The species are: *Alsmithia longipes, Clinostigma exorrhizum, Balaka seemannii, B. macrocarpa, B. streptostachys, B.* 'bulitavu', *Physokentia thurstonii, Hydriastele vitiensis* and *Veitchia filifera*.

Conservation Threat Status of Fiji's Palms

Many of Fiji's palms have restricted distributions and are threatened either because of small population sizes, forest disturbance (logging, fire, deforestation, clearance), or establishment of mahogany plantations. It is also true that the distribution of many of our palms is not fully known, so they may not be as restricted as we currently believe them to be. Until their full distribution can be documented, we need to be conservative in respect of their threat status.

The threat status now almost universally recognised is the IUCN Global Status, according to

The foothills of Mt Sorolevu in Vanua Levu, probably the richest palm forest in Fiji with at least nine species, four of which are endangered.

the 'IUCN Red List of Threatened Species'. The threat categories now used in Red Data Books and Red Lists have been in place, with continual improvement, for almost 30 years. Since their introduction these categories have become widely recognised internationally, with the Red List categories providing an easily and widely understood method for highlighting those species under higher extinction risk, so as to focus attention on the need for or efficacy of existing conservation measures. A simplified description of the categories applicable for this guide is as follows (refer http://www.redlist.org for a full description and the annually updated status):

- Critically Endangered – when a species is facing an extremely high risk of extinction in the wild;
- Endangered – when a species is facing a very high risk of extinction;
- Vulnerable – when a species is facing a high risk of extinction in the wild;
- Near Threatened – for species which are close to qualifying for or is likely to qualify for a threat category in the near future;

- Least Concern – for species which have been evaluated against and do not qualify for the criteria above. Widespread and abundant species are included in this category; and,
- Data Deficient – there is insufficient information to make an evaluation.

The currently accepted threat status of Fiji's palms follows the analysis of Dylan Fuller and Michael Doyle[8] made in 1996. The results of their analysis are summarised in Table 3 with the author's new recommendations based on improved information and updated Criteria from IUCN. In summary, 15 or well over half of Fiji's palms are threatened, six (24 percent) are categorised as Critically Endangered; four (16 percent) as Endangered, a further five (20 percent) Vulnerable; and the remaining 10 (40 percent) are Near Threatened or Least Concern.

Conservation Synopsis

There are 25 Fijian palms species currently known, and there are surely several yet to be discovered. Of these, all but one, and possibly two exceptions, are endemic to Fiji, which places the responsibility for conservation squarely on our own shoulders.

Although there would appear to be plenty of potential dispersal agents for these palms, notably birds and bats, 12 species of palm have extremely restricted distributions. These and an additional three are currently categorised as globally threatened on the IUCN Red List. While we suspect introduced rats as serious seed predators of palms, their actual role in endangering and determining the distribution of these palms remains unknown.

In contrast, it is quite clear that avoidable human activities are a serious threat to several palms. These activities are almost entirely encompassed within the jurisdiction of forest management, because all of Fiji's palms (the sago palm, a partial exception) are found only in forest and are unable to survive outside of forest except through cultivation. The most serious threats are deforestation and forest conversion to mahogany plantations. The conversion of large areas of our best lowland forest without any consideration of biodiversity impact has been particularly damaging. Added to these is the very destructive and poorly controlled mode of logging currently being practised.

Unfortunately, these impacts are in no way balanced by positive conservation efforts. The resources of our conservation institutions are poor and awareness of the status of threatened palms and forest biodiversity in general is extremely limited. Consequently, Fiji's protected area system plays an ineffectual role in forest and palm conservation, except on Taveuni, and even here management of the protected areas is essentially passive; for example, not one of the three

---

[8] Doyle, M.F. and D. Fuller. 1998. Palms of Fiji-1. Endemic, indigenous and naturalized species: changes in nomenclature, annotated checklist, and discussion. *Harvard Papers in Botany*, Vol. 3, No.1: 95-100

In the wild, the Lauan fan palm *Pritchardia thurstonii* is now restricted to a few rat-free islets, such as these in the Vulaga lagoon.

protected areas has a management plan. It is not surprising therefore that the late Dick Phillips, a man of action rather than words (though he did not hesitate to speak his mind when he thought it might do some good), made little attempt to address *in situ* conservation efforts, but was very active in pursuing *ex situ* conservation. Consequently, several of our threatened palms are now growing in secure collections overseas and in the Garden of the Sleeping Giant in Nadi, where their conservation can be assured.

However, reliance solely on this form of conservation for the threatened palms is inadequate and inappropriate in Fiji's circumstances. We still have large areas of forest and palms are suitable 'flagships' for forest conservation. Difficulties of conserving Fiji's palms probably reflect those of many of our endemic plants and animals. There is a desperate need to address these with the best methods available to us in the 21st Century. In particular, we need:

- improved knowledge of the distribution of our threatened palms and focused research on their community dynamics;

- a moratorium on the conversion of rainforest to mahogany plantation and a serious attempt to limit forest loss through fire and piecemeal conversion;
- the existing mahogany plantations to be managed to achieve 'certification' standard.
- the means to enable landowners to benefit from the establishment of mini 'protected areas' for highly endangered species;
- properly controlled logging operations which include biodiversity and palm conservation issues in their planning and execution;
- improved public awareness of Fiji's palms, their potential for landscaping and their role as flagships for forest conservation.

Species Accounts
Fiji's Indigenous Palms

Alsmithia

Named for Dr Albert Charles Smith (1906-1997), who in 1926 began his professional career with an exploratory botanical trip to South America. He subsequently turned his attention to the Pacific and made at least six botanical collecting visits to Fiji between 1933 and 1969. Between 1979 and 1991 he published the six-volume *Flora Vitiensis Nova*, a highly comprehensive account of Fiji's flora and the standard botanical reference today.

Alsmithia is a monotypic genus endemic to Fiji and quite closely related to *Cyphosperma*. Not described[9] until 1982, when it was believed to be endemic to Taveuni, but in 1996 a population was found by Dylan Fuller and colleagues on Vanua Levu.

Alsmithia longipes

Refers to the elongate 'stem' of the inflorescence and the extended petiole of the frond.

Description: A medium-sized, rather sparse-looking palm to 10m in height with a slender trunk, up to 10 cm in diameter that bears prominent, irregular nodes. The fronds, usually 8-12 in number and 3.6m in length, have a long petiole, evenly and well spaced shiny leaflets and no crownshaft. Emerging fronds are a striking pinkish-red which darkens after a few days to bronze

[9] All new species of plants are scientifically 'described' and this process gives them an official Latin name which is the basis for recognizing that plant from all others.

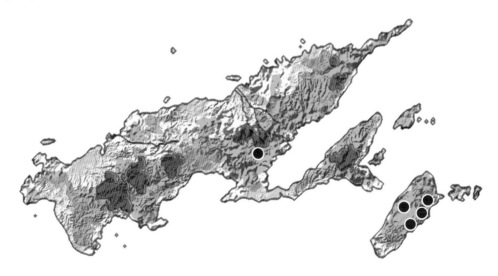

Distribution of *Alsmithia longipes*, Vanua Levu and Taveuni.

Alsmithia longipes at the edge of a forest clearing above Soqulu, Taveuni.

Mature fruit of *Alsmithia longipes*.

```
|       |     |     |     |     |
0        Alsmithia longipes (4.0cm)        5cm
```

TYPICAL FRUIT LENGTH

and then green. The inflorescence emerges between the fronds, is large and stout and the fruit are large (about 3.5 cm by 2.5 cm) and bright crimson at maturity. The fruit are strongly fragrant, a unique attribute amongst Fijian palms. The Vanua Levu *Alsmithia* has a couple of distinguishing characteristics that make it strikingly attractive – the colour of the flower stem is a rich dark red, while the flowers are bright yellow. The Taveuni form's flower stalk is whitish turning pale pink or greenish without contrasting flower buds.

Distribution: Known from four or five localities in north-central Taveuni and one locality in Vanua Levu – in the northeast foothills of Mt Sorolevu.

Habitat and Ecology: *Alsmithia* is a palm of the wettest areas of Fiji – the northern and eastern slopes of Taveuni, which has a rainfall of over 9000 mm annually. Here it is found as a sparsely distributed, understorey or forest-edge palm on gentle and steep slopes between 100-600 metres. The fragrant fruit would indicate that fruit-bats (*Pteropus* or *Pteralopex* spp) rather than birds are the likely dispersal agents.

Cultural Uses: No Fijian name or uses have been recorded.

Conservation Status: Fijian endemic. Currently classified as Endangered (IUCN Global Status) because of its restricted distribution on Taveuni and Vanua Levu. However, this should be reviewed now that three other populations on Taveuni have been found and because all but two of these are in a protected forest area – the Bouma National Heritage Park.

Balaka

From the widespread Fijian name for all the members of this genus.

Restricted to Fiji and to Samoa, where there are at least 10 species. Four are recognised in Samoa and six in Fiji, but only five are described at present. They are all small, slender, understorey palms of mature rainforest. The apical leaflets are united in a broad wedge-shape – this is a diagnostic feature of the genus, displayed by all the Fijian *Balaka* to varying degrees. Fiji's *Balaka* palms are by no means completely known. *B. longirostris* in particular appears to be a variable species while the relationship between *B. macrocarpa* and *B.* '**bulitavu**' requires clarification, as does another recently found on the Tunuloa Peninsula of Vanua Levu. A good deal of intensive work on both Viti Levu and especially Vanua Levu is required to fully understand the species we have in Fiji.

Balaka longirostris

From the long 'rostrum' or beak of the seed.

Description: A slender, straight palm to about 8m tall. Trunk is slender to 6 cm in diameter, variable colour but usually has prominent raised nodes, often blotched with lichen, moss and epiphytes. Fronds, usually 5-7 in number, are ascending to horizontally held and up to 2.5m in length. The

Distribution of *Balaka longirostris* on Viti Levu.

Balaka longirostris in the dense, wet forest north of Veisari on Viti Levu's southern coast.

Mature fruit of **Balaka longirostris** are characteristically large and scarlet.

0   *Balaka longirostris (3.5cm)*   5cm

TYPICAL FRUIT LENGTH

crown shaft is relatively inconspicuous, being narrow and green. The inflorescence emerges from below the crownshaft, is often sparse, 1-2 branched and held out horizontally or partially erect, often with a long stem. The fruit are large, 3-4 cm long and 1-1.5 cm wide and bright scarlet when mature. The seed is distinctive with sharp ridges and bearing a long projection.

Distribution: Restricted to Viti Levu where it is believed to be widespread in undisturbed forests of the wet zone, but confirmed identifications are actually restricted to no more than half a dozen locations.

Habitat and Ecology: An understorey palm, common in certain places where it may be found growing in a variety of aspects and micro-habitats – slopes, drainages and flats, but clearly requires good shade and moist to wet conditions. Has been recorded from near sea level up to 1000m.

Cultural Uses: All species of *Balaka* in Fiji are referred to by the same name, that is, are considered by Fijians to belong to the same taxon. The original Fijian name appears to have been **balakwa**, which is still used in the highlands of Navosa, possibly a compound of **ba** 'stem' plus **lakwa** 'hollow, empty', though the application of this is obscure. Derived forms such as **balaka** are used in Vanua Levu, Taveuni and parts of Viti Levu. The name **niuniu** is also used in parts of eastern Viti Levu, including Emalu in the upper Wainimala and Rewa, where the palm is remembered as being the source of spears, known as **moto belaka**. The slender stems are also used for **meke** spears, walking-sticks and are favoured clothesline props.

Conservation: Endemic to Viti Levu. Widespread in remaining forest and not believed to be threatened. Currently considered as Least Concern (IUCN Global Status).

Balaka macrocarpa

From the Greek *macro*, large and *carpus*, seed.

Description: A small palm to 8m high with a trunk from 5-10 cm diameter, conspicuous pale recent leaf nodes on green trunk but lower down, usually heavily adorned with epiphytes and moss. A compact crown of 7-12 ascending and slightly arching fronds to 2.5m in length. The fronds bear wide, well-spaced, generally erect, dark green leaflets. A bulging green crownshaft. Inflorescence emerges beneath the crownshaft, may be large and heavily laden. However, the large (3-4 cm long and 1.5 cm in diameter), orange-red mature fruit are rarely encountered. Palms under full shade are larger and more robust than those which emerge through the canopy.

Distribution of *Balaka macrocarpa.*

Balaka macrocarpa – one from the small population in the upper Nabukavesi Creek, Viti Levu.

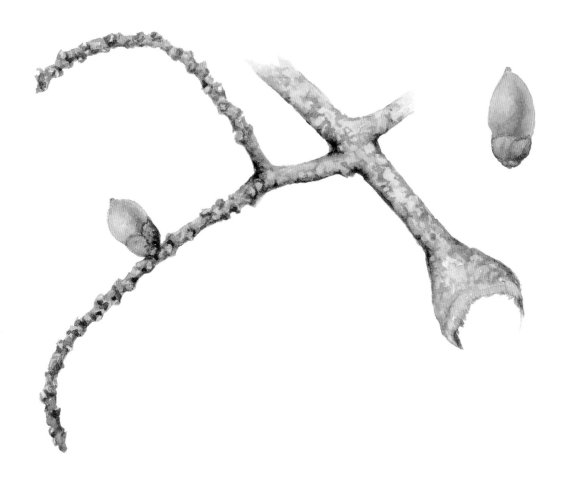

The large seeds of **Balaka macrocarpa** are heavily predated,
possibly by the masked shining parrot *Prosopeia personata*.

0   *Balaka macrocarpa (3.5)*   5cm

TYPICAL FRUIT LENGTH

Distribution: The original description is from a now unknown location on the Natewa Peninsula, Cakaudrove, Vanua Levu but the best known population of what is attributed to this species is from the upper Nabukavesi Creek catchment, Namosi on Viti Levu. Both these appear somewhat similar, but with major differences to the recently found *B.* 'bulitavu' along the Matani Creek in the northern foothills of Mt Sorolevu, Cakaudrove, Vanua Levu. Clearly these require further taxonomic work to clarify their relationship.

Habitat and Ecology: An understorey or semi-emergent palm in wet forest from about 200-400m, where it grows on slopes or drainage lines in undisturbed forest and where it may be very locally common. Regeneration in the Nabukavesi population is fair but mature fruit are very rarely encountered. The large fruit are usually predated as they approach maximum size but before ripening. The masked shining parrot *Prosopeia personata* is the likely culprit. This large parrot rarely, if ever, disperses the fruit, being a seed predator, easily opening the seed with its powerful bill and extracting the soft interior.

Cultural Uses: The names **balaka** and **niuniu** have been recorded, as well as its use for spears.

Conservation: Fijian endemic. Currently regarded as a highly threatened palm – Critically Endangered (IUCN Global Status). The field location of the original collection in the Natewa Peninsula is unknown and the two populations in the centre of the island are believed to be small. Similarly the population along the Nabukavesi Creek was estimated in 1996 at about 200 mature trees. Mahogany plantations are being established close to this population and if they are extended further, then they will pose a major threat.

Balaka microcarpa

From the Greek *micro*, small and *carpus*, seed.

Description: A small but occasionally tall and slender palm to 13m high and 8 cm diameter. The trunk is green with distinct nodes below the crownshaft, but lower down becomes grey-brown, heavily adorned with epiphytes, moss and lichen of various colours. A compact crown with 7-10 ascending fronds, to 2m in length, with large, well-spaced dark green leaflets. As with several, if not all the Balaka, the fronds are considerably longer in those palms growing in full shade than those in open areas. The crownshaft is slight and dark green with inflorescences emerging beneath it. Inflorescenses are two or three times branched with a long petiole and are often held erect. The fruit are small, oval in shape about 2 cm long by 1 cm wide, and bright orange-red when mature. Young palms are conspicuous, with characteristic entire leaves. The transition from the entire leaf to the pinnate form occurs on average after the 28th leaf.

Distribution: Known from only one population in the forests immediately north of Suva, Viti Levu.

Distribution of *Balaka microcarpa*, Viti Levu.

Balaka microcarpa in the Coloisuva Forest Park, near Suva.

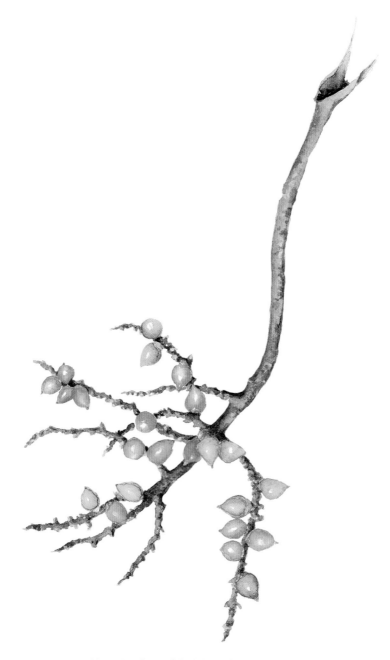

Maturing fruit of *Balaka microcarpa.*

```
┌─────────────────────────────────────────────┐
│  0        Balaka macrocarpa (2.0cm)      5cm  │
└─────────────────────────────────────────────┘
```
TYPICAL FRUIT LENGTH

Habitat and Ecology: An understorey, rarely semi-emergent palm of the wet forests of Coloisuva and Savura Creek at an altitude of 50-300m with an annual rainfall in excess of 4000 mm and with no dry season. In the early 1980s, Dr Julian Ash of the University of the South Pacific made a detailed ecological study of this palm over a three-year period and found it to be very slow growing with palms maturing at about 5m in height when they would be about 45 years old. Flowering and fruiting occurs throughout the year. The oldest palm he observed was estimated to be 85 years. Annual fruit set is very variable with about 180 fruits on each inflorescence each year. Only about 0.1 percent of these fruit survive to become a mature palm. No observations were made on seed dispersers, so gravity and water are believed to be the main agents.

Cultural Uses: The Fijian name **balaka** has been recorded.

Conservation: Endemic to Viti Levu. Although quite common where it occurs, this is a very limited area of about 10 square kilometres. Nearly the entire population is located in one of several adjacent reserves – the Coloisuva Forest Park (wholly a mahogany plantation), the Savura Forest Reserve (about 75 percent mahogany plantation), the Vago Forest Reserve (mature forest) and the Tamavua and Savura Watercatchment Reserve (mature forest). However, about half of this distribution is under planted mahogany (Coloisuva and Savura Forest Reserve). Clearly the felling of the mahogany which has commenced will have a major impact on this palm unless it is undertaken with great care everywhere and the major palm locations are left intact. The current threat category is Endangered (IUCN Global Status) but in view of the ongoing mahogany felling and clearance for agriculture elsewhere, this should be revised to Critically Endangered.

Note: *Balaka pauciflora* described from material collected by the U.S. Exploring Expedition (1840), purportedly from Ovalau, is now believed to be an early collection of *B. microcarpa*. This is according to Dylan Fuller who made an extensive search of Ovalau in 1995 and found no *Balaka* nor any Ovalau villagers who knew of a palm fitting its description.

Balaka seemannii

Named for Berthold Carl Seemann, 1825-1871, a noted German botanist and the author of *Flora Vitiensis* [1865-73]. Seemann was born and educated in Germany, moving at the age of 19 to England, where he became a gardener at Kew. He was selected to be the botanist on a British Government Mission, led by Colonel William J. Smythe, to consider the proffered cession of Fiji in 1860. Seemann's assignment was to advise on the native and cultivated plants of Fiji and the suitability of potential crops. He was in Fiji for only six months but managed to travel widely. Not only did he prepare a detailed and highly favourable recommendation to accept cession, but he put together an enormous collection of botanical specimens – over 1000 in all – which he subsequently worked up for publication as *Flora Vitiensis*, which became the standard botanical reference for Fiji's flora until the 1970s and is still consulted today.

Description: A small, elegant palm to 8m high, with a slender, greyish often blotched trunk to 5 cm in diameter and with prominent nodes. Quite often grows at an angle or lying against an adjacent sub-storey shrub or young tree, very occasionally decumbent. A rather sparse crown with 6-7 ascending fronds to 1.5m in length, which bear widely-spaced, dark green leaflets and a slight green-brown crownshaft. A quite large and wispy inflorescence emerges beneath the crownshaft. The small, ellipsoid fruit are bright red at maturity, 1.5-2 cm long and slightly beaked.

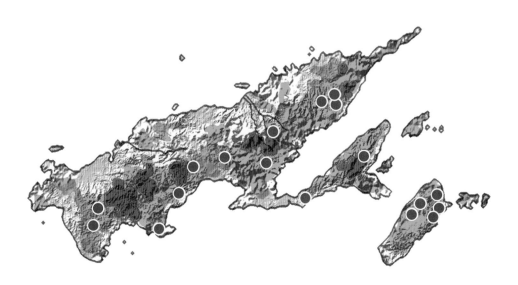

Distribution of *Balaka seemannii* in the forests of Vanua Levu and Taveuni.

Balaka seemannii in the remaining forests of the Natewa Peninsula, Vanua Levu.

Balaka seemannii fruits profusely with small, cherry red fruit.

0   *Balaka seemannii (1.8 cm)*   5cm

TYPICAL FRUIT LENGTH

Distribution: Widely distributed in the forests of Taveuni and Vanua Levu.

Habitat and Ecology: *B. seemannii* is the most tolerant of all the *Balaka* of different forest types, being found at high elevations (over 900m) in forests with over 8000 mm of rain a year, but also in mature seasonal forest of intermediate zone vegetation, at lower altitudes with approximately 3000 mm of rain a year.

Cultural Uses: The most common use today of the *Balaka* is as a walking stick with the slightly expanded base, shaved and polished to form a very attractive handle to be cupped in the palm of the hand. Also the favoured species for traditional **meke** (dance) spears. More than any of the other members of the genus, this species is best known as **balaka**. Medicinal properties have been reported for this palm, the bark being used to treat headache and the pericarp of the fruit used to treat venereal disease, while the leaves and roots are reported to show microbial activity.

Conservation: Fijian endemic. A common palm for which there is no conservation concern at the present time, currently categorised as Least Concern (IUCN Global Status).

Balaka streptostachys

From the Greek *strepto*, twisted and *stachys* in reference to the intermittent twists in the middle of the inflorescence stem.

Description: The stoutest of all *Balaka* with a trunk to 10 cm in diameter and 4-7m tall. Also distinguished by the unique twists of 40-60° in the rachilla (inflorescence stem) with the sections between the twists otherwise straight, a character not observed in other *Balaka* species. The trunk is green but turns grey with age, the nodes are conspicuous, light green-brown. The crown comprises 8-10 fronds to 3m in length, held erect, with regular quite closely spaced leaflets which are mid-green in colour, while the crownshaft is green-light brown. The inflorescence emerges between the leaves in young palms and beneath the crownshaft as they get older. The inflorescence is branched to three orders with the characteristic twists described above. The fruit are orange-red at maturity, averaging 22 mm long and 11 mm wide.

Distribution: Known from a single site on the northern foothills of Mt Sorolevu, Vanua Levu.

Habitat and Ecology: An understorey palm in wet, lower montane forest. The sole known population is restricted to a site above the Matani Creek, with an annual rainfall of over 3000 mm.

Cultural Uses: No Fijian name or uses reported.

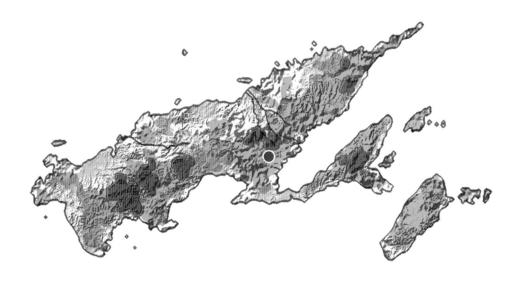

Distribution of *Balaka streptostachys* and *Balaka* bulitavu,
both of which are known only from the one location on Vanua Levu.

Balaka streptostachys is the latest *Balaka* to be described and is known only from a single population in the foothills of Mt Sorolevu, Vanua Levu.

Conservation: Endemic to Vanua Levu. The only known population comprises 50-60 adult trees, which are vulnerable to ongoing logging activities. There are reported plans for conversion of the area to mahogany plantation – a highly precarious situation for this palm, which is considered Critically Endangered (IUCN Global Status).

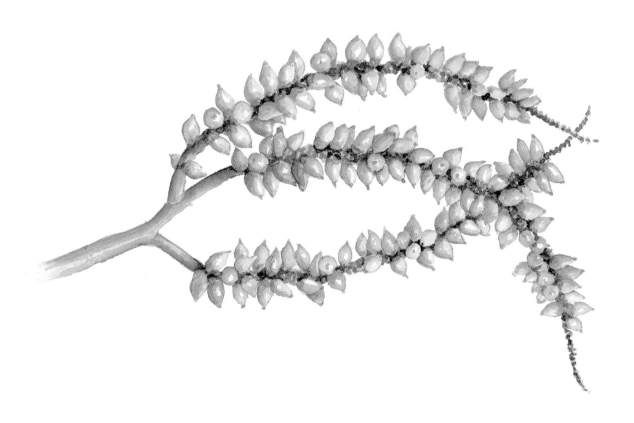

Maturing fruit of *Balaka streptostachys*, a surprisingly small fruit from this, the largest of the *Balaka*.

0   *Balaka streptostachys (2.2cm)*   5cm

TYPICAL FRUIT LENGTH

Fiji Balaka Seeds

(ACTUAL SIZE X 2)

Balaka longirostris

Balaka 'bulitavu'

Balaka longirostris

Balaka macrocarpa

Balaka longirostris

Balaka microcarpa

Balaka seemannii

Balaka streptostachys

The seeds of Fiji's **Balaka** palms are distinctive. Except for **Balaka seemannii**, all have up to five prominent ridges. **Balaka longirostris** has a variable number of ridges. Three species have an elongated rostrum of varying size at one end. When mature, the fruit of all the **Balaka** have a thin coating of soft pulp that soon rots off when they fall to the ground.

Balaka sp. 'bulitavu'

Description: A distinctive, small *Balaka* reminiscent of *B. seemannii* but with enormous fruit, larger even than the fruit of *B. macrocarpa*. Trunk to 6m tall and 3-4 cm in diameter. A sparse crown with 4-6 fronds to 1m in length, with 4 or 5 widely spaced leaflets and distinctive fused terminal leaflets. Prominent, slightly bulging crownshaft. Juvenile leaves may be entire with a deep terminal notch on palms nearly 2m tall. The inflorescence is infrafoliar and once branched. Bears the largest fruits of all Fiji's *Balaka*, 4-5 cm long and 2-2.3 cm wide, bright orange when mature. The seeds are 4 cm long, sharply ridged and keeled, scalloped with a pronounced beak, similar to *B. longirostris*.

Distribution: Known only from a single population in Vanua Levu on the northern foothills of Mt Sorolevu (refer distribution map with *B. streptostachys*).

Habitat and Ecology: An understorey palm in wet, lower montane forest, found in association with *B. streptostachys*.

Cultural Uses: Villagers from Satulaki village referred to this palm as **balaka** and did not distinguish it from *B. seemannii*.

Conservation: Endemic to Vanua Levu. The only known population may comprise 100-200 adult trees, although there has been little searching beyond the immediate vicinity of the site. As with *B. streptostachys*, this area is vulnerable to logging activities and reported plans for conversion to mahogany plantation. A precarious situation for this Fiji palm, which is also considered Critically Endangered (IUCN Global Status).

Balaka 'bulitavu' is the smallest in stature of the *Balaka* but the fruit are certainly the largest.

This delightful little *Balaka* 'bulitavu' has not yet been scientifically described or officially named.

0 *Balaka 'bulitavu' (4.5cm)* 5cm

TYPICAL FRUIT LENGTH

Balaka sp. 'natewa'

Description: A *Balaka* with a distinctive juvenile form is found on the Natewa Peninsula in Vanua Levu. Adult *Balaka* close by are superficially similar to *B. macrocarpa* but no mature fruit have been collected to confirm this. Since the original collection and description of *B. macrocarpa* was made from Natewa material, it would seem likely that the distinctive juvenile is indeed this species; however, *B. macrocarpa* at Nabukavesi on Viti Levu has no such distinctive juvenile form. *B. macrocarpa* is the only *Balaka* found on both Viti Levu and Vanua Levu and with the recent finding of *B.* '**bulitavu**' and this poorly known *B.* '**natewa**', all of which are superficially similar, there is clearly a need to clarify the relationships between these species or forms.

This form is so poorly known that it is not listed as a distinct taxa at present.

An unusual juvenile *Balaka* 'natewa' from Navonu in the Natewa Peninsula, Natewa Bay.

Calamus

From the Latin *calamus*, a reed or cane, referring to the slender, cane-like stems of these palms.

A very large genus of over 380 species extending from Africa, South Asia, Sri Lanka to its centre of diversity in Southeast Asia, to Papua New Guinea, Australia, Solomon Islands, Vanuatu, with the sole Fijian species being the easternmost outpost in the Pacific. As a group these palms are collectively called rattans and they are in great demand for cane furniture.

Calamus vitiensis

From the Fijian name for Fiji, Viti.

Description: A climbing palm with a slender, spiny stem. The fronds are feathery with finely divided leaflets to 2m; the rachis bears recurved hooks which are particularly well developed on the

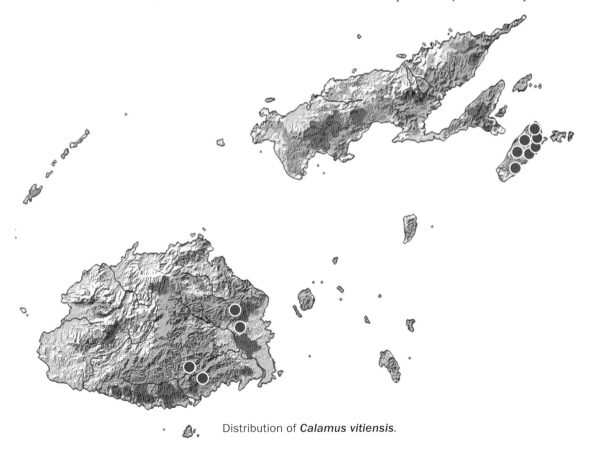

Distribution of *Calamus vitiensis*.

Calamus vitiensis emerging from the forest canopy on a karst limestone outcrop at Wailotua, Tailevu.

Borne high in the canopy, the small but attractive fruit of *Calamus vitiensis* are rarely seen.

0   *Calamus vitiensis (1.0cm)*   5cm

TYPICAL FRUIT LENGTH

cirrus (whip-like tip of the frond to 1.5m), which is otherwise bare and may be nearly as long as the frond itself. The hook-armed cirrus is an efficient aid for climbing and collectively they enable the palm to climb rapidly through to the canopy. The lower section of the thin cane trunk is bare, with persistent dead leaves in the central section and live fronds only over the top few metres. The inflorescence is a prominent structure, long and tough, arising from within the leaves and bearing the flowers on small curling branches. It may reach 2m in length (shorter in males), branched to four times. The fruit are white when mature, scaly in appearance and almost spherical about 1 cm in diameter. This palm is dioecious, meaning there are separate male and female plants.

Distribution: Until recently, this palm was considered an endemic Fijian species; however, the species limit is now recognised as including others in Vanuatu, the Solomons and Queensland.[10] Traditionally, Taveuni is always thought of as the homeland of **qanuya** in Fiji, and it grows there in profusion, more so than anywhere else. However it is also found but not common in the highlands of eastern Viti Levu – Namosi, Waidina, Wainimala, Wainibuka, though it is quite common on the limestone hills around Wailotua. It is reported but not confirmed from Qamea off Taveuni and also the windward forests of Vanua Levu – Dama, Bua and Nakobo, Cakaudrove.

Habitat and Ecology: On Taveuni it grows most commonly in disturbed forest in open, exposed locations, but is also found in mature forest on steep slopes. On Viti Levu, it is far less common and its distribution is peculiarly restricted for unknown reasons. Here it occurs mainly in mature forest.

Cultural Uses: Until fairly recently, the name **qanuya** would instil fear into the heart of any Fijian, for it was not only the standard name for this rattan, but also for the rattan cane that was the favoured means of castigation by schoolteachers, **turaganikoro** (village headmen), sergeant-majors and so on. In today's more enlightened times, the word is unlikely to be recognised by most Fijians. **Qanuya** is the name on Taveuni, while on Viti Levu it is known by three related words: **wataburakitaci** (Namosi), **wataburaitaci** (Waidina, Wainimala), and **wataburreitaci** (Wainibuka). The origin of this name could be 'the vine that blocks the view of the ocean' – something which its scarcity on Viti Levu today does not justify. Another name recorded from around the source of the Wainimala river is **warusi**.

Although never used by Fijians for furniture (an unsuccessful cottage industry was started with foreign assistance on Taveuni in the 1980s), this rattan is everywhere regarded as a useful vine for a variety of domestic and construction uses.

Conservation: Not considered threatened in any way. The intriguing question is why is it so common on Taveuni and relatively rare on Viti Levu (and even more so, if it actually occurs, on Vanua Levu). Currently categorised as Least Concern (IUCN Global Status).

---

[10] Baker, W., Ross Bayton, John Dransfield and Rudi Maturbongs (2003). A Revision of the *Calamus aruensis* (Arecaceae) complex in New Guinea and the Pacific. *Kew Bulletin* 58: 351-370.

Clinostigma

From the Latin words *clino* meaning bend or recline and *stigma* meaning spot or mark.

A western Pacific genus of about 11 species ranging from the Bonin Islands, Japan to Samoa.

Clinostigma exorrhizum

From the Latin *exo* (outside) and *rhizum* (roots), referring to the exposed, stilt-like roots which emerge at the base of this palm as it grows in size and maturity.

Description: This is a very distinctive palm. A tall palm with a moderately stout, pale grey-brown trunk to 20m in height. Characteristic spiny, bronze-brown prop roots, 1-2m long at the base.

Distribution of *Clinostigma exorrhizum*.

Usually found only on cloud-covered ridges at high elevation,
this *Clinostigma exorrhizum* is located near Des Voeux Peak on Taveuni.

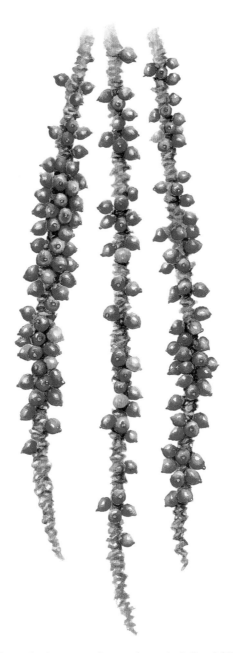

Large fruiting bunches of minute seeds are characteristic of **Clinostigma exorrhizum.**

0 *Clinostigma exorrhizum (0.5cm)*   5cm

TYPICAL FRUIT LENGTH

Mosses and epiphytes tend to cover the trunk. The crown holds about 12 fronds to 6m in length, held horizontally with many fine drooping leaflets. A long and prominent, light green crownshaft. A distinctive inflorescence emerges from the base of the crown, initially being held out horizontal before becoming pendulous. The inflorescence may be branched to three orders but with long parallel stems; these are white initially, becoming green as small fruit develop. The fruit are ovoid about 5 mm long, and translucent red when mature. The late Dick Phillips noted that two fruiting stalks he obtained provided about 14,000 seeds.

Distribution: Quite widespread, with several well dispersed populations on Viti Levu and Vanua Levu; all over the high forest on Taveuni and with a small population on Gau.

Habitat and Ecology: A palm of the cloud-covered high forests where it occurs on ridge tops and steep slopes – usually as a conspicuous emergent of upper montane and cloud forest. Usually found well above 700m, but as with other 'upper montane forest' elements considerably lower where persistent cloud and misty conditions enable it, for instance down to 250m at Waisoi in Namosi and on Gau island, at about 500m. On Vanua Levu, there is a small population at Wainika at about 50m above sea level in apparently normal lowland rainforest. This is truly divergent from its normal habitat.

Cultural Uses: Although the name **niusawa** has been recorded for this palm, it properly refers to other species. Elsewhere the generic **niuniu** is used. **Qavio** is a genuine name recorded only for this species – from Dogotuki, Vanua Levu and over the watershed at Wainika, Cakaudrove, **qavio** and **qavio damu** is also used. The inflorescence, once dried, makes a fine besom broom and these are still used today in Vanua Levu. At Wainika, the extraordinary lowland population of **qavio damu** is well known to the local community and the hill where it is found, Drokavia, is a sacred site, about which the community relate a variety of legends of giants and warfare. An album of traditional songs entitled *Qavio damu ni Drokavia* has been released by a local group.

Conservation: Fijian endemic. There are some large populations of *Clinostigma* with over 1000 palms in at least two areas on Viti Levu – Monasavu and Namosi, as well as a similar number or more on Taveuni. These population numbers, combined with the high altitude requirements of this palm where there is less deforestation pressure, mean that there is little overall conservation concern for this palm at the moment. The exception is the population on Gau where the numbers appear to be no more than 50. The lowland population at Wainika, Vanua Levu appears superficially to be typical, but it is such a divergent habitat for this species that it should, perhaps, be looked at more closely. Overall the current categorisation is Least Concern (IUCN Global Status).

Cyphosperma

From the Greek *kyphos*, bent or humped, and *sperma*, seed – referring to the furrowed and ringed seeds.

A small Southwest Pacific genus of five species (one undescribed) with three in Fiji, and one each in Vanuatu and New Caledonia. Formerly, the Fijian members of the genus were placed in *Taveunia* – derived from Fiji's third largest island.

Cyphosperma tanga

From the first reported Fijian name for this species.

Description: A moderately stout, small understorey palm to 5m tall and 15 cm in diameter. Chocolate-brown trunk. About 12 characteristic large, undivided or occasionally split, fronds held rather erect, to 3m long. No crownshaft. Old leaves often persisting around the trunk, overall a rather tattered appearance. The green inflorescence is long and sparse to 1.5m in length and branched to two orders. It emerges from between the leaves and is initially erect before becoming pendulous. The fruit are oblong ellipsoidal, yellowish-brown when mature, up to 1.4 cm long.

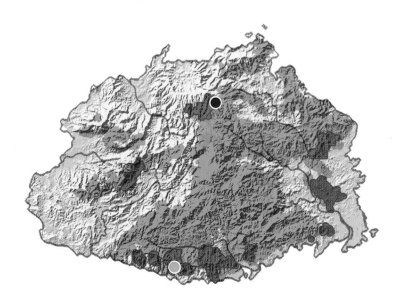

Distribution of **Cyphosperma tanga** in red and **Cyphosperma** 'naboutini' in blue.

Cyphosperma tanga from the small population restricted to a single site
on the western slopes of Mt Tomaniivi, Fiji's highest mountain.

Distribution: A highly restricted distribution – a single population around the Dromodromo Creek on the slopes of Mt Tomanivi, Viti Levu, Fiji's highest mountain.

Habitat and Ecology: An understorey palm on rocky volcanic soils, sparsely distributed on steep slopes in montane rainforest at an altitude of 600-900m on the northwestern slopes of Mt Tomanivi. High rainfall of over 5000 mm annually with little seasonality.

Cultural Uses: None reported. Navai villagers call this palm **taqwa**, which in Nadroga and some parts of Navosa is applied to *Veitchia joannis*. The name 'tanga' from which the specific name is derived, is an attempt at anglicisation.

The Navai community relate a story on the origin of this palm: *"At a time long ago, two chiefs, who were twins, were travelling through the Navai-Nasoqo area. They had with them a special* tabua *(sperm whale's tooth) which was wrapped in a large undivided leaf of the* taqwa *palm. Stopping to rest for a while, they decided to bury their special* tabua *in its wrappings, before proceeding on their way. Subsequently, a* taqwa *palm grew up from the buried tabua and is today found only at this one site, which is called Vunitabua (literally 'tabua tree')."*

Conservation: Fijian and Viti Levu endemic. This is one of the most threatened of Fiji's palms. It is regrettable that one of the two known populations of this palm was destroyed by logging and the establishment of a plantation, despite some vociferous complaints by the late Dick Phillips. A survey in 1995 by Dylan Fuller showed that the only extant population numbers about 300-400 adult trees, and fortunately that regeneration in this population is reasonable. This palm is categorised as Critically Endangered (IUCN Global Status).

Notes:

Cyphosperma trichospadix

From the Greek *tricho*, hairy and *spadix*, branch referring to the stems of the fruiting cluster.

Description: A moderately stout palm to 7m tall with a 'shiny' green-brown trunk, up to 8.5 cm in diameter. Although sometimes described as having a crownshaft, this species is similar to the other two forms in Fiji with short, clasping leaf bases. The fronds are up to 2.5m in length with 7-10 in a spreading crown; they are divided with normal, closely-spaced pinnate leaflets 2m long. The inflorescence emerges from between the fronds, erect at first but eventually hanging down. It is long and sparse to 1.5m. The fruit are ovoid, but bulging slightly on one side, up to 2 cm long, a dirty yellow-white at maturity.

Distribution: Found on the islands of Vanua Levu (one confirmed location currently known, Mt Mariko) and a single location on Taveuni near Lake Tagimoucia.

Habitat and Ecology: An understorey palm in high elevation forest from 600-1100m altitude in areas of very high rainfall – 7000-10,000 mm on Taveuni.

Cultural Uses: None known.

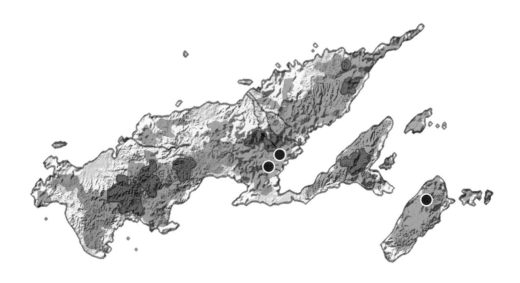

Distribution of *Cyphosperma trichospadix*, Vanua Levu and Taveuni.

Cyphosperma trichospadix, a single palm found on the trail from Somosomo village to the fabled Lake Tagimoucia, Taveuni.

Conservation: Fijian endemic. The distribution of this palm is still poorly known but it does occur on two islands and appears to survive, sparsely distributed in at least two and perhaps many separate locations. It is currently categorised as Vulnerable (IUCN Global Status).

Maturing fruit of **Cyphosperma trichospadix**.

0   Cyphosperma trichospadix (1.8cm)   5cm

TYPICAL FRUIT LENGTH

The fruit of **Cyphosperma** 'naboutini' have proved difficult to procure.

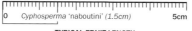

0   *Cyphosperma* 'naboutini' *(1.5cm)*   5cm

TYPICAL FRUIT LENGTH

Cyphosperma sp. 'naboutini'

Description: In appearance, unlike *C. tanga* but a little more like a slender version of *C. trichospadix* because of its fully divided leaves. The fronds, 7-12 in number, are up to 2m in length, with a bare petiole to over 50 cm and relatively thin, closely-spaced leaflets. Slender, brown-green trunk to 5m often with the old fronds persisting around it. The inflorescence emerges between the leaves and is long and sparse, erect at first and then hanging down. The fruit are small (up to 1.5 cm) and dull purplish-red when mature.

Distribution: Known only from a single population in lowland forest at Naboutini, Serua on Viti Levu (refer Distribution map of *C. tanga*). Here it is restricted to at least four adjacent drainage lines in one water-catchment.

Habitat and Ecology: An understorey palm of lowland rainforest.

Cultural Uses: None reported at the present time and no local name.

Conservation: Fijian and Viti Levu endemic. Together with *C. tanga*, this is likely to be Fiji's most endangered palm. Formerly known from a single population of about 50 palms in a logged-over forest area, subsequently planted to mahogany. The first rotation of the mahogany was felled in 2003, causing considerable damage, including mortality, to a number of the trees. However, a landowner-based conservation initiative is concentrating on defining the distribution of the palm and ensuring that ongoing logging by the community does not damage more palms. This is being led by Peceli Tuisawau, son of the chief of the landowning clan, who has taken a keen interest in the conservation of this palm. The surveys to date have located another three small populations in undisturbed forest along creeks within the same watershed.

It is indeed ironic and disturbing that the establishment of mahogany plantations, something for which Fiji is internationally famous, is heavily implicated as a major threat to the very existence of Fiji's two most endangered palms (as well as several others – see *Hydriastele vitiensis*, *Balaka microcarpa* and *Balaka macrocarpa*). It is an issue which the Fiji Hardwood Corporation will need to address seriously in the near future, in order to avoid the wrath of the international conservation community. Fortunately, the interest and involvement of Peceli Tuisawau and the Namaqumaqua landowners is a significant positive development for this unique palm.

Currently, this palm is categorised as Critically Endangered (IUCN Global Status). The final determination and description of this palm requires a full collection of all the various parts of the palm, especially the flowers and fruit, which is being undertaken at the current time.

Lucky to survive, the only known population of **Cyphosperma** 'naboutini'
is nestled alongside creeks in the Naboutini mahogany plantation, southern Viti Levu.

Heterospathe

From the Greek *heteros,* different or of another kind and *spathe,* the bract enclosing an inflorescence in bud – combined in reference to the different manner in which the two bracts enclose the inflorescence.

A widespread genus of about 37 species of the tropical western fringe of the Pacific (Philippines, Micronesia, eastern Indonesia, Papua New Guinea, Solomon Islands and Vanuatu), with the exception of the single species recently described from Fiji. First recognised as a distinctive, new palm by the late Dick Phillips and grown for many years in his Suva garden, the palm was described in 1997.

Heterospathe phillipsii

Named for the late Dick Phillips (1923-1999), horticulturist and Fiji's pioneering palm specialist.

Phillips' Palm

Description: A solitary and generally slender palm to 15m in height. The trunk may become quite stout, to 20 cm in diameter, but is usually less than 15 cm, and develops a pronounced bulbous base. The fronds are light, feathery and graceful with numerous leaflets; they reach 5m in length and arch in a curve to below the horizontal and lack a crownshaft. Dead fronds, or frond bases, may

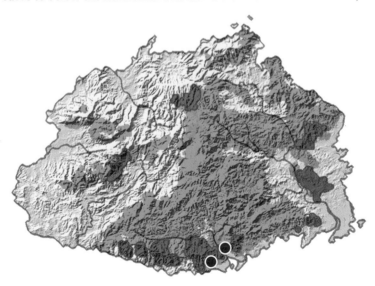

Distribution of ***Heterospathe phillipsii****,* Viti Levu.

Heterospathe phillipsii, named for the late Dick Phillips,
who pioneered interest in Fiji's palms.

Small bright red fruit of *Heterospathe phillipsii*.

0   *Heterospathe phillipsii (1.2cm)*   5cm

TYPICAL FRUIT LENGTH

persist on the trunk, giving it a tattered appearance. When emergent the crown becomes much more compact, with 10-12 fronds. The inflorescence is large and wispy, branched to two orders, with small dispersed fruit (a little over 10 mm long) which are bright crimson when mature.

Distribution: Known only from three small, restricted populations on Viti Levu – one near Nakavu, inland from Navua, the site of the Natural Forest Management Project, the second on the immediate western side of the Navua River, and the third inland from Deuba. Also reported from the Nukurua area in Tailevu, but this population has not been confirmed and the area is now under mahogany plantation.

Habitat and Ecology: Occurs sparingly in and on the edge of dense lowland rainforest as an understorey, canopy or semi-emergent palm. These forests are some of the wettest in lowland Fiji. Masked shining parrots have been recorded eating the fruit.

Cultural Uses: The only Fijian name recorded for this rare palm is the generic **niuniu**. The palm heart is edible and the immature seeds are eaten; they are reported to taste like coconut.

Conservation Status: Fijian and Viti Levu endemic. Currently classified as Endangered (IUCN Global Status) because of its very restricted distribution in two small, vulnerable forest areas.

Hydriastele

Derived from the Greek *hydrias* 'nymph' and *stele* 'column or stem', the literal translation is nymph-stem but the meaning is a little obscure.

As a result of recent detailed systematic examination of four palm genera, *Gulubia*, *Gronophyllum*, *Hydriastele* and *Siphokentia*, they have been re-classified and placed in a more broadly defined genus, *Hydriastele*.[11] Unfortunately, microcarpa, the widely-known species name for the Fijian palm, is 'occupied' by the type species name for the former genus *Gronophyllum*, and this has precedence. Consequently a new name was required for this palm and *H. vitiensis* was chosen. As currently accepted, *Hydriastele* comprises 47 species distributed from Sri Lanka to Fiji.

[11] Baker, W.J. and A.H.B. Loo (2004). A Synopsis of the Genus *Hydriastele* (Arecaceae). *Kew Bulletin*, 59, 61-68.

Distribution of **Hydriastele boumae**.

Hydriastele boumae from the ridge below Mt Koroturaga, Bouma, Taveuni.

Hydriastele boumae

Boumae from latinised Bouma – the district where it this palm is found and named in recognition of the forest conservation efforts of the Bouma community.

Description: Similar in nearly all respects to *H. vitiensis* but differs in at least two readily observable attributes. Most noticeably the fronds of the immature sub-canopy palm remain undivided or very weakly divided, while the cylindrical fruit are much larger and bulkier, 1.3 by 0.7 cm.

Distribution: Occurs only on Taveuni where it was originally found as a small population in the hills above Soqulu Estate, on the central-western side of the central divide. Recently a much larger but quite restricted population has been found in the Bouma district around Mt Koroturaga in the north where it occurs in large numbers from about 100-800m on the ridges leading up to the summit.

Habitat and Ecology: Conspicuous as a strongly emergent palm very similar to *H. vitiensis*, it occurs in tall lowland forest right up to the highest ridges with a canopy height of no more than 10-12m. Its habitat is considered the wettest in Fiji with an annual rainfall of between 7000-10,000 mm. Rain-laden clouds cover the ridges down to 300m for most of the time.

Its restricted range is somewhat puzzling, especially when on one occasion within a period of 20 minutes, three birds were seen taking fruit and flying off – the barking pigeon (*Ducula latrans*), Taveuni's fabled orange dove (*Ptilinopus victor*) and the Polynesian starling (*Aplonis tabuensis*). With this many potential dispersal agents, it is surprising that it is not found all over the island.

Cultural Uses: None known. The villagers of Vidawa in Bouma refer to this palm by the generic **Niuniu**.

Conservation: Fijian and Taveuni endemic. Given the large population on Mt Koroturaga and its foothills, and the possibility of other populations elsewhere in the highest and wettest parts of Taveuni – areas which are unlikely to be disturbed because of the climate and the steep slopes, this palm must be considered secure. More especially because the landowners of the area, the Vanua of Bouma, have set up the Bouma National Heritage Park and are actively promoting ecotourism in the area. Indeed the guided hike from Vidawa village takes walkers past several stands of this *Hydriastele*, as well as *Alsmithia longipes*, *Calamus vitiensis*, *Balaka seemannii* and *Veitchia simulans* – while higher up the hill can be found *Clinostigma exorrhizum* and *Physokentia thurstonii*, a veritable feast of Fijian palms. Currently categorised as Data Deficient but with the new information available will be proposed as Least Concern (IUCN Global Status).

Mature fruit of **Hydriastele boumae.**

0   *Hydriastele boumae (1.3cm)*   5cm

TYPICAL FRUIT LENGTH

Characteristic entire leaves of a juvenile **Hydriastele boumae** from forests above Vidawa village, Bouma, Taveuni.

    This is Fiji's most recently described palm, mid-2004. Considering how common this species is within its restricted range and how conspicuous it is on the high ridges of northeast Taveuni, it is surprising it has not been noticed by the many palm experts, enthusiasts and botanists who have travelled down the road to Bouma and Lavena to see *Alsmithia longipes*, or other species. However, Taveuni's forest and ridges are usually covered in cloud or draped in mist, when it is not raining. In 1980, when the late Dick Phillips took the renowned palm taxonomist Harold Moore to Lavena to collect a new palm that became *Alsmithia longipes*, they were greeted by the destructive cyclone Tia. They managed to locate and collect the new palm but had no time or inclination for further palm exploration, even though this undescribed species was growing on the ridges all around them.

A sole *Hydriastele boumae* on the ridge above Vidawa village, Bouma, Taveuni.

Hydriastele vitiensis *(formerly Gulubia microcarpa)*

Vitiensis from latinised *Viti* – the Fijian name for Fiji; *microcarpa* from the Greek *micro*, small and *karpos*, fruit.

Description: A distinctive tall palm which may grow to over 25m in height with a smooth, slender grey-brown trunk to 30 cm in diameter. The crown, with 20 or more fronds, is distinctive with strongly arched fronds and erect leaflets, giving it a compact, round appearance. The fronds are up to 2.5m in length. The palm has a prominent, rather bulbous light green-brown crownshaft and the inflorescence emerges below this. The inflorescence is compact and horse tail-like, a creamy-yellow colour, branched to two orders and held horizontal. The immature fruit are reddish, becoming yellowish-white when mature; they are small, the size of a grain of rice, no more than 10 mm long and cylindrical with a slight curve.

Distribution of *Hydriastele vitiensis*.

An emergent *Hydriastele vitiensis* on the ridge above Naboutini, Viti Levu.

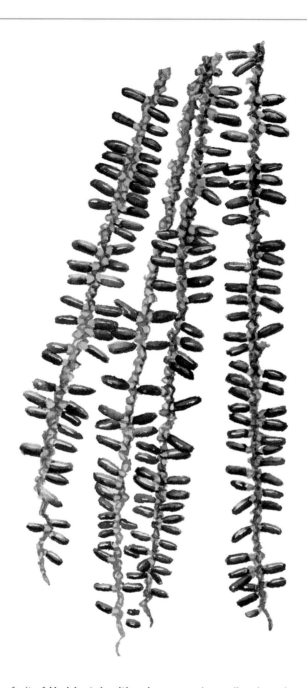

The fruit of **Hydriastele vitiensis** are much smaller than those of **H. boumae**.

0   *Hydriastele vitiensis (0.9cm)*   5cm

TYPICAL FRUIT LENGTH

Distribution: Originally described from a small area inland from Galoa, Serua on high ridges of Viti Levu's southern mountain chain which separates the upper Navua River and the coast. Recently it has been found that this population extends eastwards across the Navua River at several sites on the continuing mountain chain up to and including Mt Nakobolevu, overlooking Suva City. In 1995, it was also discovered for the first time on Vanua Levu, at two locations in Cakaudrove, Mt Sorolevu at 570m altitude and inland at 25m altitude at Wainika on Udu Point.

Habitat and Ecology: A conspicuous emergent, usually on ridges, and often rising strongly from the canopy in small colonies. The original population was found on forested hill ridges at 300-400m, although all this area has now been converted to mahogany plantation. Some of the palms have survived the transition. The more recently discovered populations on Viti Levu remain in undisturbed or logged-over forest on similar ridge-lines at around 300-600m. The Vanua Levu populations occupy similar ridge-top situations, but the altitudinal limits here are from near sea level to 570m.

Cultural Uses: No specific name has been reported, only the generic **Niuniu**. The palm heart is reported to be edible.

Conservation: Currently categorised as Vulnerable (IUCN Global Status) because of its likely small population size, despite the quite large number of small disjunct populations which are found on two islands.

Metroxylon

From the Greek *metra*, heart and *xylon*, wood – referring to the pith in the trunk which is extracted as a source of food in some species.

A small genus of seven species indigenous to the Pacific. Believed to have originated in New Guinea, where there are two species, with one each in Fiji, Samoa, Vanuatu, the Solomon Islands and the Caroline Islands. Widely cultivated and naturalised throughout the Pacific region and Southeast Asia. Sago starch from the trunk pith of one species is a very important food staple for many communities in Southeast Asia and New Guinea.

Distribution of *Metroxylon vitiense* (red) and the introduced *Metroxylon warburgii* (blue), with two unknown populations (black).

Metroxylon vitiense in a typically thick and untidy stand near Galoa village, Viti Levu.

Metroxylon vitiense

From latinised *Viti* – the Fijian language name for Fiji.

Fiji sago palm

Description: A large conspicuous palm to 15m in height. A single thick brownish trunk, usually with a tattered appearance through the persistence of dead fronds. An arching crown with erect fronds to 5m in length; the frond bases bear wickedly long spines in neat rows. No crownshaft. At maturity, after about 15 years, this palm produces a large, twice-branched inflorescence to 4m in height. A large number of flowers are produced, and over a period of 12-15 months these develop into fruit. The attractive fruit are large (5-7m in diameter), brown with light scalloping, a distinctly scaly appearance and feel. By the time the fruit fall, all the fronds have died and fallen back; the palm dies thereafter. (Refer also *Metroxylon warburgii* page 151.)

Distribution: Probably endemic to Viti Levu and Ovalau (a landbridge island off Viti Levu), because there is only one confirmed occurrence on Vanua Levu which is a small stand. *M. warburgii* appears to be more widespread on Vanua Levu than Viti Levu but nowhere are there large stands similar to those which remain on Viti Levu. Reported from Rotuma, but these are likely to be *M. warburgii*. In southeast Viti Levu large stands occur at the back of coastal swamps at Navua, Taunovo Bay and Galoa, but also found in the Rewa delta and inland in isolated localities in the Rewa catchment. A large and very interesting stand occurs on either side of the upper Navua River gorge. On Vanua Levu, there is a small stand outside Savusavu at Valaga Bay.

Habitat and Ecology: Clearly thrives only in swampy habitats but even so has a very restricted range on Viti Levu. In the remaining four or five locations at the back of the coastal plains on the south coast, this palm forms dense, almost monospecific stands. In contrast, the unique forest assemblage above the upper Navua River gorge comprises dense palm stands in the myriad of short, flat water courses with large numbers also occurring up-slope, mixed with typical lowland forest tree species.

The fruit of **soga** (the Fijian name for the palm) are large and float, and are generally thought to be dispersed by water, but in the upper Navua gorge, half-eaten fruit away from bearing palms indicate another dispersal agent and the large, endemic masked shining parrot is suspected.

Cultural Uses: The most widespread Fijian name is **soga** and there is no relationship whatsoever with the similar English name sago which is derived from the Malay-Indonesian *sagu*. The Fijian word **soga** is probably derived from **coga** meaning 'thorn', with reference to the thorns that distinguish the soga from other Fijian palms. The other Fijian name – **niusoria**, used in parts of Ovalau – probably has a similar origin, being composed of **niu** 'palm' and **soria**, another word

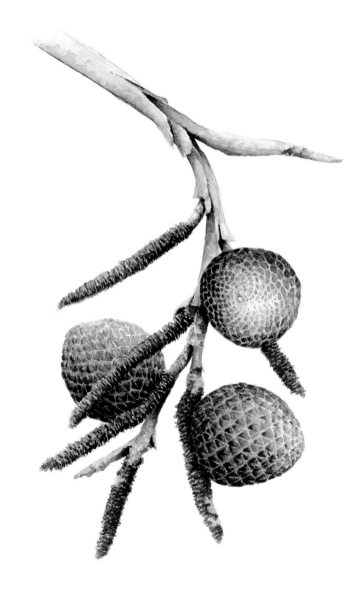

Characteristic large scaly fruit of **Metroxylon vitiense.**

Metroxylon vitiense (9.0cm) 0 10cm

TYPICAL FRUIT LENGTH

meaning 'thorny' or 'prickly'. All the evidence is that **soga** has never been used as a source of starch by Fijians or eaten for its 'palm heart'. However, it is much sought after today by the local Indian community for its 'palm heart'.

In contrast to Fiji, in many parts of Papua New Guinea and the Solomons sago is a staple food, and its use as a food was also known in parts of northern Vanuatu and even in Rotuma. In all these places, and more, it is also a standard thatching material, and indeed its local names indicate it is often synonymous with the word for 'thatch'. In Fiji, however, although it is today a much sought after thatching material as it has been for the past century, it is quite likely that its use as such was learned from Solomon Islanders brought to work in Fiji, as indeed the people of Deuba explicitly told the anthropologist Geddes.

The origin of the sago palm in Fiji remains the subject of considerable debate and interest. The apparent restriction of the palm to Viti Levu and the lack of any evidence of its use for thatch or as a starch staple, points to sago being a relatively late and accidental arrival in Fiji. In contrast, its ancient origin in Fiji is supported by its biological status as a distinctive species and the results of pollen analysis from peat swamps which found that in about 4000 BP (ie before human arrival to Fiji) the **soga** was abundant in the Rewa River delta and perhaps in other delta areas. The pollen analyses indicated that it retreated quickly to its present restricted distribution soon thereafter, and this led to the suggestion that this was a result of increasing exploitation as a food staple. This is not, however, supported by any cultural record of **soga** as a food source in Fiji, and recent analyses have shown that **soga** has one of the more fibrous trunks of all the *Metroxylon* species, and as such is an unsuitable food source. Together, these suggest it is unlikely that it was ever used for food, and that its distributional retreat may have been due to changing hydrology of the coastal plains with increasing human modification for root crops and/or with delta and coastal configuration changes resulting in the gradual establishment of the extensive peatlands which are not attractive **soga** habitat.

Noted Fijian linguist Dr Paul Geraghty provides further linguistic evidence of a recent arrival for sago. He believes it is possible that the earliest name for sago actually survives in Fijian, but refers not to sago but to another starch-bearing plant. The earliest name for sago among the ancestors of the Fijian people was **rambia**, which was used by the speakers of Proto-Oceanic, a language believed to have been spoken in the New Guinea region some 3500 years ago. The word is lost in the Solomon Islands, has one cognate in Vanuatu, and reappears in Fiji as **yabia**. In Fiji, however, the word refers not to sago but to a totally different plant, one which is also a source of starch – arrowroot *(Tacca leontopetaloides)*.

If sago had been known to the earliest settlers of Fiji, it would almost certainly have been known by the name **yabia**. The fact that the name **yabia** was transferred to another plant is, in Geraghty's opinion, strong evidence that sago was not present during the early human occupation of Fiji. However, just to extend the perplexity with the sago-**yabia** relationship, today the largest remaining stand of sago is in Serua behind Wainiyabia village, which, using this terminology, means 'sago palm river'. This is certainly not arrowroot habitat, so is this purely a coincidence?

Conservation Status: Fijian endemic. Vulnerable (IUCN Global Status). Today, there is an increasing use of **soga** from the remaining stands at Deuba and Galoa, Viti Levu, for 'heart of palm', a practice which kills the tree. There is no monitoring of this trade and it is doubtful if it is sustainable. Some villagers and residents in the area say that the stands have decreased greatly in area. As such this trade poses a threat to this restricted range endemic species, and the 'heart of palm' trade should be discontinued and transferred to a cultivated situation or different species altogether.

Neoveitchia

From the Latin *neo*, new. Literally 'new' *Veitchia*, referring to the previously described genus *Veitchia*.

Since the genus *Neoveitchia* was first described in 1920, this singular palm was considered to be a monotypic genus endemic to Fiji, but in 1994 a closely related species was discovered in Vanuatu.

Neoveitchia storckii

Named for Jacob Paul Storck (1838-93), a botanical collector and assistant of Berthold Seemann on his assignment in Fiji. Storck was born in Germany but took a job with the Sydney Botanical Gardens, where he met Seemann on his way to Fiji in 1860 and became his assistant. After Seeman's departure the following year, Storck remained in Fiji for the rest of his life but maintained contact with him and sent him botanical specimens at Kew Gardens, London, from time to time. Storck was an industrious planter, especially of cotton and sugar, and he also introduced many crops to Fiji. His plantation at Viti on the Rewa River was a model of its time.

Description: A solitary, moderately stout palm with a light-coloured trunk on an expanded base. Trunk normally to 12m in height and stout, at about 25 cm in diameter, but may be up to 20m

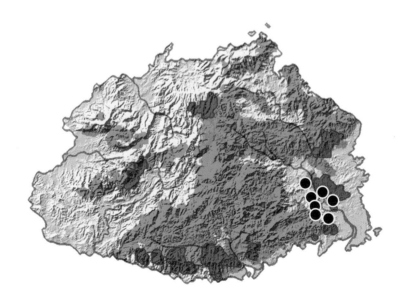

Distribution of **Neoveitchia storckii**, Viti Levu.

A lone *Neoveitchia storckii* in secondary forest near Naqali, Viti Levu.

Characteristic tassles below the fruit of *Neoveitchia storckii*.

0   *Neoveitchia storckii (5.5cm)*   10cm

TYPICAL FRUIT LENGTH

when growing under a high canopy of plantation mahogany. A full, leafy canopy of 12-15 fronds per crown; fronds up to 5m long with heavy leaflets and a characteristic lateral twist to 90°. The crownshaft is distinctive, being incompletely formed and a glossy dark green to black. A bulky inflorescence arises below the crownshaft, initially white before turning olive-green. Fruit mature only on the basal third of the fruiting stem, the remainder forming conspicuous white tassels. The fruit are large, up to 5 cm long and 2.5 cm in diameter, dull red when mature.

Distribution: Formerly believed to be restricted to a small area of secondary forest near Naqali in central Viti Levu, but Dylan Fuller and associates showed that it was in fact more widespread, with a discontinuous population, covering more than 50 km^2 on the western side of the Rewa River. More recent observations have found it on the eastern bank of the Rewa River too, surviving in the extensive mahogany plantations of Nukurua, Tailevu.

Habitat and Ecology: An emergent palm which grows in the alluvial plains of the middle Rewa River and the nearby rolling foothills. Much, if not all of this, is secondary forest and undergoing steady clearing for agriculture while the eastern bank of the Rewa is a major mahogany plantation. *Neoveitchia* survives quite well in open areas and degraded forest.

Cultural Uses: The Fijian name appears to be **vilaito** (but often referred to in the literature as **vuleito**), though overall it is not well known and its origin is obscure. The immature fruit are reported to be eaten like gum and the trunks were used for house posts.

Conservation: Fijian and Viti Levu endemic. In 1971, Suliana Siwatibau and her co-workers found this palm only as a single population in an area of less than 2 hectares. At the time it was being attacked by the rhinoceros beetle which had largely decimated coconut plantations on Viti Levu. The beetle was subsequently controlled, but not eliminated, by the release of a biological control agent in the mid-1970s and this may have allowed *Neoveitchia* to recover to its present, safer conservation status. However, in the author's garden, this species is still attacked by the occasional rhinoceros beetle. It is classified as Endangered (IUCN Global Status).

Physokentia

From the Greek *physa*, bellows or bubble, and *kentia* after the British landscape gardener William Kent. Combined, referring to the swollen and bubbly appearance of the endocarp.

A Southwest Pacific group of seven species from the Bismarck Archipelago, Solomon Islands, Vanuatu and Fiji. Recently, the taxonomic status of a 'lost' monotypic palm from Fiji – *Goniocladus petiolatus* – was resolved and found to be *Physokentia rosea*, which had to be renamed, as *petiolatus* had precedence over *rosea*.[12]

[12] Fuller, Dylan 1999. The lost palm of Fiji, a resolution of *Goniocladus*, and a preliminary cladistic analysis of *Physokentia. Mem. New York Bot. Gard.* 83:203-212.

Distribution of **Physokentia petiolatus** (red) and **Physokentia thurstonii** (blue).

A small stand of juvenile *Physokentia petiolatus* on Gau Island.

Physokentia petiolatus (formerly *Physokentia rosea*)

Petiolatus from the Latin, referring to the stem; *rosea*, for the red coloured rachilla and flowers.

Description: A moderate palm to 8m with a dark green trunk bearing conspicuous leaf scars, although these are often covered with moss and epiphytes. The most characteristic feature is the prominent cone of prickly, occasionally branched, stilt roots which replace the main trunk completely (not the case in *Clinostigma exorrhizum*), these roots may extend to well over 1m in height and 5 cm in diameter and bear a reddish papery tip. The fronds, usually 8-10 in number and up to 2m long, spread horizontally or curve slightly with only slightly drooping, bright green leaflets. There is a prominent green-grey crownshaft. The inflorescence emerges from beneath the crownshaft, is twice branched and relatively compact. The flowers (both sexes) are deep pink to red in bud, turning to green as the fruit form. The fruit are round, to 2 cm in diameter, shiny red and becoming black at full maturity.

Distribution: Generally considered to be restricted to Viti Levu, but also occurs on Gau Island where a small population persists in the cloud-covered forests around Mt Delaco. On Viti Levu mainly found on the upper montane forest areas around Nadarivatu, Tomaniivi and the Rairaimatuku Plateau, and also sparingly at lower altitudes (300-400m) on the southern coastal mountain chain where similar humid, high rainfall conditions exist. An outlier population occurs at the Nakauvadra Range.

Habitat and Ecology: On Viti Levu occurs mainly at altitudes of between 750-1250m but on coastal mountains and on Gau occurs at lower altitudes. In most situations, an understorey palm but when occurring on ridges or in some of the low stature vegetation on the Rairaimatuku Plateau it becomes sub-emergent and sometimes fully emergent. On Gau, the island thrush *Turdus poliocephalus* has been observed feeding on the fruit of this palm.

Cultural Uses: There are two old names reported – **tagadanu** and **tana** (both probably refer to **taqa** or **taqwa** as used for other small palms in the area, with the suffix **damu** – red).

Conservation: Fijian endemic. Quite common in the Tomaniivi Nature Reserve and the recently established and adjacent Wabu Reserve, as well as in the water-catchment of the Monasavu Dam which is currently informally protected. Consequently, its conservation status should be secure. On Gau, the population is small, perhaps in the low hundreds, and the recent construction of a telecommunications tower without any impact assessment or enquiry as to the conservation values of Gau's very small area of low altitude 'cloud forest' demonstrates the vulnerability of this unique habitat. Thus the isolated populations on Gau island of both this species and *Clinostigma exorrhizum* are very vulnerable. Categorised as Near-threatened (IUCN Global Status).

Mature fruit of *Physokentia petiolatus.*

0   *Physokentia petiolatus (2.0cm)*   5cm

TYPICAL FRUIT LENGTH

Physokentia thurstonii

Named for Sir John Bates Thurston (1836-1897), who made the type collection, that consisted only of fruits. Thurston was a planter, horticulturist and keen amateur botanist, and he established the Botanical Gardens in Suva, later to become Thurston Gardens. Thurston arrived in Fiji at Rotuma where he was shipwrecked, subsequently acquiring a cotton plantation on Ovalau before settling in Taveuni. He was elected to the Legislative Assembly and then became Prime Minister in Seru Cakobau's government. Thurston played a leading role in the cession to Britain, served as Colonial Secretary and then Governor of Fiji.

Description: Similar to *P. petiolatus*. A medium palm to 7m. Trunk a strong green with prominent light leaf scars, usually greyer below with moss and lichen. Characteristic occasionally branched, stilt roots. A crown with 8-10 spreading fronds with broad, bright green leaflets held horizontally. At their base, these form a robust olive crownshaft up to 60 cm in length. A twice-branched inflorescence emerges from beneath the crownshaft; the fruit are roundish, up to 2.5 cm in diameter and shiny black at maturity.

Distribution: Occurs on Taveuni and Vanua Levu and appears to be quite widespread on both islands.

Habitat and Ecology: Similar to *P. petiolatus*, principally an understorey palm of the high forests and hill crests, but it is clear that this species descends to much lower elevations than does *P. petiolatus*. On Vanua Levu it has been found down at about 300m near Vatuvonu and in the foothills of Mt Sorolevu, both in Cakaudrove.

Cultural Uses: The only reported name is the generic **niuniu**. A decoction of its leaves is reported to be useful in treating heart trouble.

Conservation: Fijian endemic. Widespread on both Vanua Levu and Taveuni and in places common, especially at high elevations which are less likely to be impacted by logging, deforestation and agricultural expansion. Currently, categorised as Near-threatened (IUCN Global Status), but probably a candidate for Least Concern status.

A tall *Physokentia thurstonii* from the forest above Vatuvonu, Vanua Levu.

Pritchardia

Named for William Thomas Pritchard, first British Consul to Fiji, 1858-63. Pritchard was born in Tahiti and educated in the UK, before returning to join his father, the British Consul in Samoa. In Samoa, he acquired an exceptional knowledge of Polynesian language and traditions, and an understanding of Pacific Islanders' customs and culture – probably a rare attribute for a British diplomat at the time. It is not surprising, therefore, that when appointed the British Consul to Fiji he launched himself wholeheartedly into the affairs of the country. He castigated planters, cancelled unfair land sales, intervened in Fijian quarrels and warfare and reproofed and got the better of the hitherto unassailable Tongan warlord, Ma'afu. He received the offer of cession and was a great proponent of colonial expansion. But for circumstances, probably beyond his control, Pritchard might have been hailed the Stamford Raffles of the Southwest Pacific. Instead he was discredited, dismissed, all but dishonoured and met his fate, in unknown circumstances, at the hands of native American Indians. Berthold Seemann was Pritchard's greatest admirer and he named this palm for him.

A true Pacific islands palm consisting of about 28 recognised species, 22 of which are endemic in the Hawaiian Islands. The remainder are found in Southeast Polynesia, Cook Islands, Samoa, Tonga and Fiji. Aboriginal introductions are found in Vanuatu and the Solomon Islands and recently these fan palms have become internationally widespread in landscape gardening.

Pritchardia pacifica

From the Latin *pacificus*, peaceful, but referring to the geographic location, the Pacific Ocean.

Fiji fan palm

Description: A very handsome and well-known palm with roundish leaves, divided at the edge, that may be one metre in diameter. The palm may grow to 15m in height but is usually less than this, the trunk pale grey-brown, fairly stout when grown on open ground but much slenderer when grown in thick vegetation or under a canopy. Several inflorescences emerge from between the leaves; they are branched to three orders and are borne on a pronounced petiole with the flower-fruit cluster at the tip. The fruit are round, 10 mm in diameter and purplish-black when mature.

Distribution: There is no consensus as to where this palm originally came from, though Tonga, rather than Fiji or Samoa is generally preferred. In Fiji, this palm is widely cultivated throughout the islands, but is not found away from existing or former village sites. The situation is similar in much of Tonga and Samoa, though in Tonga it is found in eastern forest areas of 'Eua where it appears to be indigenous. On the Rotuman island of Uea, this palm grows in what is now mature forest. House mounds on the island indicate that it was inhabited at some point long ago.

Typical situation – a mature *Pritchardia pacifica* in a Fijian village.

Mature fruit of **Pritchardia pacifica**.

0   *Pritchardia pacifica (1.0cm)*   5cm

TYPICAL FRUIT LENGTH

Habitat and Ecology: Its natural habitat is not known.

Cultural Uses: Known internationally as the Fiji fan palm. In Fijian culture, the fan palm is valued as an ornamental, traditionally found mainly in the vicinity of chiefly houses. The fans made from their leaves (**irimasei**) used to be carried only by chiefs as an insignia of their rank, but nowadays they are most commonly used in fan dances (**meke wesi**). They are also used opportunistically to serve as a protection from both the sun and rain. In respect of the latter, it explains the name of the fan palm becoming the name for an umbrella. The most widespread name for the fan palm is **masei**. In certain Lauan islands it is called **iviu** which is derived from what is believed to be a much more widely used form, simply **viu**. In Nadroga it is called **roro**, while on the Natewa Peninsula, parts of Vanua Levu, Taveuni and northern Lau it is **sakiki**. In Rotuma, the palm is called **fakmaru** and its seeds are commonly eaten.

There are interesting linguistic clues which indicate that this palm may have occurred more extensively in Fiji previously. The name fan palm in much of western Polynesia is **piu**, which seems to have been borrowed from the old Fijian name for it, **(i)viu**; while the Tongan word for a fan made from the leaf of the **piu** used in traditional dance is **sakiki**, which is taken from the name for the fan palm in parts of Vanua Levu and northern Lau. Similarly, the Rotuman name **fakmaru** is borrowed from **fakamalu**, the Tongan word for umbrella. Thus linguistic evidence seems to indicate that the fan palm was originally absent (or present only in insignificant quantities) in western Polynesia and Rotuma, or perhaps was present in earlier times but subsequently lost and then re-introduced from Fiji.

Although the majority of *Pritchardia* palm species are in Hawaii, it is more probable that the genus originated in the western Pacific, perhaps Fiji itself, based on the proximity of related native species while the Hawaiian species may be of fairly recent derivation.

Conservation: Questionably an indigenous Fijian palm. Its landscape and cultural use maintains this species. It is not found in the wild in Fiji, so its conservation status has not been analysed.

Pritchardia thurstonii

Named after Sir John Bates Thurston – refer *Physokentia thurstonii*.

Lauan fan palm

Description: An attractive palm which is very similar to *P. pacifica* and from which it can be distinguished by two easily observed characters, but only on mature palms. Only a single inflorescence arises between the leaves in this species, whereas in *P. pacifica* there can be two or three. The inflorescence is branched to three orders, but comprises a compact head on a stalk over 2m long which extends well clear of the fronds, while in *P. pacifica* the stalk is shorter than the fronds. The round fruit of *P. thurstonii* are small (6-7 mm) and red-black, while those of *P. pacifica* are larger (9-11 mm) and purple-black at maturity.

Distribution of *Pritchardia thurstonii*.

Pritchardia thurstonii on an islet in the lagoon at Ogea, Lau Group.

The mature fruit of **Pritchardia thurstonii** are slightly smaller than those of **Pritchardia pacifica**.

0   *Pritchardia thurstonii (0.6cm)*   5cm

TYPICAL FRUIT LENGTH

Distribution: Confined to three island clusters – Vanuabalavu, Vulaga and Ogea in the Lau Group. On Vanuabalavu it occurs only in the Sovu islets, while in Vulaga and Ogea, it is restricted to small coralline islets in their respective lagoons, being absent from the mainland or from the larger islands there.

Habitat and Ecology: Restricted to uplifted coralline limestone islands, where it can grow in profusion and to the almost complete absence of other plants.

Cultural Uses: In Vulaga and Ogea, southern Lau, **leva** is the generic name for fan palms. *P. pacifica* is distinguished by the name **levawai** 'water (or weak) leva', and *P. thurstonii* by **levavatu**, meaning 'stone (or strong) **leva**', possibly because it grows on limestone islands. Where it occurs, it has similar uses to *P. pacifica*, although the people of Vulaga in southern Lau record using the long inflorescences of this species for snaring the blue-crowned lory *Vini australis* to use its brilliant feathers as fringes for their finest mats. Presumably in Vanuabalavu, the same could have been done to snare the even more desirable red-feathered kula or collared lory *Phygis solitarius*, whose distribution does not extend down to Vulaga.

Conservation: Fijian endemic. Because of its very restricted and fragmented distribution and small population numbers, this palm is categorised as Vulnerable (IUCN Global Status).

It is of interest that while this palm is noted as coming from the three Lauan islands of Vanuabalavu, Ogea and Vulaga, it is actually absent from the main islands of what are in fact island groups, but survives only on small lagoonal islets. There are plenty of areas on the main islands which are just as rugged, exposed and inhospitable as the smaller islets and there is an abundance of apparently more suitable habitat, but they do not occur on these large islands, except where they have been transplanted. Why? The culprit may well be rats. It is possible that rats, which are not native to the oceanic Pacific islands, feed on the seeds and prevent regeneration. The small islets have either never been colonised by rats or they cannot support permanent rat populations, enabling the palms to persist. If rats are a major predator of *Pritchardia* seeds, this might explain why *P. pacifica* has disappeared from Fiji and why one rarely if ever sees regeneration near growing palms, and elsewhere in Polynesia (Hawaii excluded) why the remaining fan palms are highly endangered relics. The earliest colonisers of the Pacific islands brought the small Polynesian rat *Rattus exulans* with them and in doing so may have destroyed fan palm communities throughout Western Polynesia.

Veitchia

Named for John G. Veitch or his brother James, 19th century English nurserymen. John Veitch visited Fiji in 1865 to collect plants of horticultural potential and interest, some of which were subsequently grown back in England.

Currently eight species of *Veitchia* are recognised with four each in Vanuatu and Fiji; one of the latter is an aboriginal introduction to Tonga. Until the recent work of Scott Zona and Dylan Fuller,[13] a further five species of *Veitchia* had been described in Fiji, but these have now been attributed to either *V. filifera* or *V. vitiensis*.

Veitchia filifera
Derived from Latin and meaning thread-bearing.

Description: Since this species now encompasses three other previously described species (*V. petiolata*, *V. pedionoma* and *V. sessilifolia*), it is not surprising that it is a somewhat variable species.

---

[13] Zona, S. and Dylan Fuller. 1999. A Revision of *Veitchia* (Arecaceae – Arecoideae). *Harvard Papers in Botany* 4(2): 543-560.

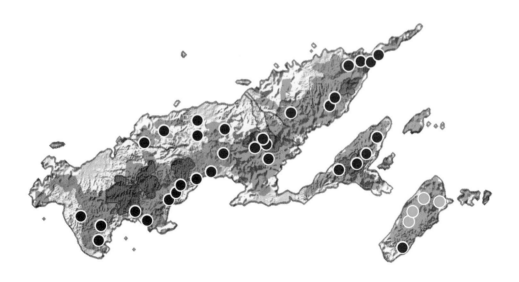

Distribution of **Veitchia filifera** (red) and **Veitchia simulans** (blue) on Vanua Levu and Taveuni.

Veitchia filifera in remnant forest area near Rokosalase, Macuata, Vanua Levu.

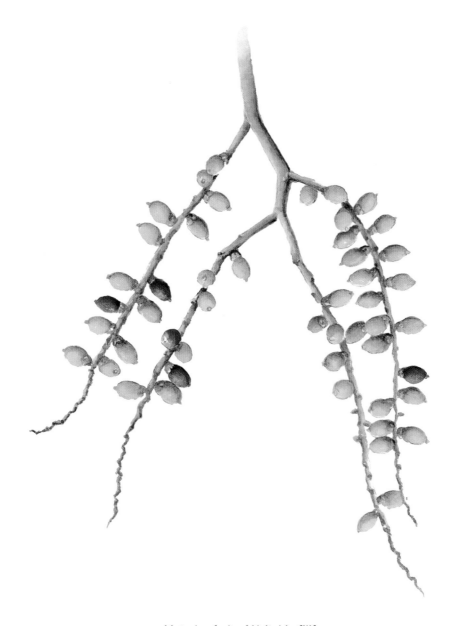

Maturing fruit of *Veitchia filifera*.

0   *Veitchia filifera (1.5cm)*   5cm

TYPICAL FRUIT LENGTH

A slender to moderately robust palm up to 15m tall and 5-20 cm in diameter, with or without a slightly expanded base. Usually with 7-12 fronds up to 2.5m in length; a prominent crownshaft which is usually dark green to brown black, sometimes with light green scalloping or mottling; leaflets dark green erect or horizontal. Dead fronds occasionally persist on the palm, hanging down by the trunk. A bulky inflorescence up to a metre in width emerges from below the crownshaft. The fruit are roughly cylindrical, usually 11-19 mm in length, yellow-orange to light red when mature.

Distribution: With the exception of a collection from the south end of Taveuni, this species is confined to Vanua Levu where it is very widespread in remaining forest, and is abundant in some locations.

Habitat and Ecology: A semi-emergent and canopy species in all forest types between sea level and 700m. It appears to grow as well in undisturbed mature forest as in disturbed forest patches.

Cultural Uses: Berthold Seemann, who first collected this species in October 1860, recorded the Fijian name **cagicake**, which he erroneously claimed to mean 'above the wind' and this has been repeated by most botanists since. Other names recorded are the generic **niuniu** (commonly), **cagicagi** and **nesi** in Bua. No uses have been recorded for this palm but the author witnessed an interesting use of the dead but not fallen fronds of this palm while researching for this book. Caught out in the forest late one evening and with a one-hour walk back to the village, the villagers from Vatuvonu, Cakaudrove, collected several fronds and the resin from the **Dakua** *Agathis vitiensis*. Using a slender forest vine, they bound the fronds tightly together with the leaflets laid alongside the stem and crushed resin sprinkled through the fronds as these were being bound. This was then lit and with occasional replenishment provided a surprisingly long-lasting torch with sufficient light to get us back to the village on a moonless night.

Conservation: Fijian endemic. As with *V. vitiensis*, there is no concern about the conservation of this species as currently constituted. Least Concern is proposed for this species (IUCN Global Status).

Veitchia joannis

Named for John G. Veitch.

Description: A very tall, slender palm which can grow to over 35m. A smooth, light grey-brown trunk with a slightly expanded base, appears almost white at a distance. A graceful crown of 10-12 arching fronds up to 3m long, with drooping dark green leaflets. Characteristic of the *Veitchia*, the spear leaf appears tall and prominent, and there are usually long pendant reins. The inflorescence emerges beneath a prominent pasty grey-green crownshaft, is branched to three or four orders, and then develops large clusters of beaked red fruit (5-6 cm long).

Distribution of **Veitchia joannis**.

A characteristic group of emergent **Veitchia joannis**, off the King's Road, Tailevu.

Distinctive fruit of *Veitchia joannis* – large, with an angled projection at the distal end.

| 0 | *Veitchia joannis* (5.5cm) | | 10cm |

TYPICAL FRUIT LENGTH

Distribution: Very widely distributed throughout Fiji, with the possible exception of the southern Lau Group. Viti Levu, Vanua Levu, Taveuni, Kadavu, Gau, Koro, Ovalau, Moturiki, Moala, Totoya, Matuku, Vanuabalavu and probably many other islands. Found from sea level to 800m elevation.

Habitat and Ecology: Occupies a wide habitat range and may be found as an emergent in mature rainforest, but more often in areas of secondary forest and often associated with long-abandoned villages or settlements. In fact its wide distribution is almost certainly man-induced. Most often occurs on valley floors or alluvial plains but commonly found on steep slopes and rounded hill tops, but rarely on high exposed ridge tops. Shows a wide tolerance of soil type. In certain localities, such as Keiyasi, Sigatoka Valley, occurs on exposed limestone karst, probably associated with old hill forts, while in the Rewa delta may be found close behind mangrove areas.

Cultural Uses: This conspicuous palm has a variety of local names. It is known as niusawa in Serua, Beqa, Bau, Lomaiviti, parts of Naitasiri, Cakaudrove and Lau. The meaning of **niusawa** is nothing to do with 'red palm' as originally reported by Berthold Seemann and repeated by subsequent botanists, but means something like 'bitter palm', referring to the taste of its kernels, eaten while the fruit is still green and soft. Various places report that the heart (**torau** or **dora**) is eaten, usually raw, and the trunk is split and has been used for rafters, walls of pigpens, canoe decks and house floors. The leaves have been used for thatch and the large spathes are commonly used by Fijian children as sledges.

Another name, **sakiki**, which is used for *Pritchardia pacifica* in Natewa, Taveuni and Northern Lau, refers to this palm in the Yasawas, Lautoka, Ba, Navosa and parts of Bua. In Nadroga the name is **taqwa**, while in Vugalei, Verata, Wainimala and most of north-east Viti Levu the name is **saqiwa**. In Kadavu it is **roro** or **niuroro**. The generic name **niuniu** is also applied to it in many places.

This is the totem tree of the people from Kumi in Verata where it is called **saqiwa**, and for those who trace their origin back to Kumi but are now living elsewhere, e.g. Sote (Vugalei) and many other places in eastern Viti Levu but including communities in Kadavu, and Namuka in the Lau Group.

Conservation: Fijian endemic. One of the few Fijian palms for which there is clearly no question of conservation concern and so it is classified as Least Concern (IUCN Global Status).

Veitchia simulans

From the Latin *similis*, meaning resembling another.

Description: A medium palm with a dark grey-green trunk to 15m tall and up to 17 cm in diameter. Usually only eight or nine fronds up to 2.5m in length, these are more graceful than *V. vitiensis* and *V. filifera* because of the apparently smaller, more numerous and closely spaced leaflets. The crownshaft is very dark – green-black, sometimes with greyish mottling. Emerging from beneath the crownshaft, the inflorescence is bulky and pale, eventually bearing a large number of small yellow-orange fruit, more egg-shaped than cylindrical and 10-15 mm in length.

Distribution: Restricted to Taveuni where it is believed to be widespread but nowhere common, possibly in all mature forest areas up to at least 900m.

Habitat and Ecology: An understorey/sub-emergent palm which is poorly known. Possibly more common in the wetter forests, at altitude on the leeward side but down to nearly sea level in the wetter windward coast. Does not appear to colonise secondary forest areas. One palm authority has indicated that this species is probably more closely related to the *Veitchia* of Vanuatu or even *Carpentaria* of northern Australia than to the Fijian *Veitchia*.

Cultural Uses: Nothing recorded other than a name – **niusawa**.

Conservation: Endemic to Taveuni. In the mid-1990s logging was initiated on Taveuni and it was considered to be a threat to this species; fortunately this ceased quite quickly and the threat removed. Currently considered to be Vulnerable (IUCN Global Status), though this is a very poorly known species and Data Deficient might be more appropriate. However, it should be under no threat given the presence of three large protected areas on Taveuni – the Ravilevu Nature Reserve, Taveuni Forest Reserve and the Bouma National Heritage Park.

Veitchia simulans beside a stream above Vidawa, Taveuni.

Veitchia vitiensis

From *Viti*, the Fijian name for Fiji.

Description: A highly variable palm, with fruiting individuals varying in trunk height from about 3m to nearly 20m and diameter of 5 cm to 15 cm. The crown is usually quite characteristic, rather sparse because of the relatively few fronds, usually seven or eight, but sometimes up to 10, to 3m long, ascendant and arching but becoming pendant when older. Contributing to the sparse

Distribution of **Veitchia vitiensis**.

Veitchia vitiensis is common in the forests at Waivaka, Namosi.

Maturing fruit of **Veitchia vitiensis**.

0   *Veitchia vitiensis (1.5cm)*   5cm

TYPICAL FRUIT LENGTH

appearance of this palm is the relatively wide spacing between the leaflets. The leaflets themselves are erect when young and appear to have been severed before the tip. The crownshaft is prominent, a variable grey-green, though often with darker scalloping or mottling. A bulky, four times branched inflorescence emerges from below the crownshaft, the fruit are variable in size but much smaller than *V. joannis*, roughly cylindrical averaging 15 mm by 6 mm. As with all the *Veitchia*, hanging 'reins' are often conspicuous. These are a narrow ribbon of material which binds the spear leaf and as it unfurls, hanging loosely from the base of the frond.

Distribution: The commonest palm of the Fiji bush on the islands where it occurs, *V. vitiensis* can be found from near sea level to 1200m on the islands of Viti Levu, Ovalau, Beqa and Kadavu.

Habitat and Ecology: A semi-emergent or canopy palm, *V. vitiensis* is mostly found in mature forest but may be found in areas of secondary and logged-over forest, and in forest patches of the intermediate zone. It can be very common but is overall patchy in occurrence.

Cultural Uses: The generic **niuniu** is commonly applied to this palm. In fact, it seems likely that **niuniu** might be the original name for the similar-looking small species of *Veitchia*, *V. vitiensis*, *V. filifera*, *V. simulans*. Other recorded names are **kaivatu**, **sakiki** and **niu sakiki**. The heart is edible but as with all Fijian palms is rarely, if ever, eaten by Fijians today.

Conservation: Fijian endemic. A Fijian palm for which there is no conservation concern, currently categorised as Least Concern (IUCN Global Status).

Species Accounts

Naturalised Palms in Fiji: Ancient and Recent Introductions

Ancient Introductions

Two species of exotic palm, now naturalised in Fiji, are considered to have been brought to the islands by some of its first human colonists; those species are the ubiquitous coconut *Cocos nucifera* and the sago palm *Metroxylon warburgii.*

Cocos nucifera

Coconut and its relatives in other European languages go back to Spanish *coco* grinning face, grimace or the Portugese *quoque* monkey, with reference to the three 'eyes' at the end of each coconut which make it look like an eerie or monkey-like face. The botanical species name means bearing nuts from the Latin *nux* nut and *ferre* bring, carry, bear.

Coconut Palm

The Coconut in Fiji: Synonymous with sandy tropical beaches, the coconut palm needs no description – it is familiar to us all, as it occurs throughout the islands. While mainly a coastal plant, it will grow at altitudes over 1000m. However, fruiting deteriorates quite rapidly with altitude and it hardly fruits at all above 400m.

Origin of the Coconut: The coconut is found or has been found on most sandy coastlines of the tropics around the world. There has been a great deal of discussion, considerable romantic invention, heated controversy and even more, over its origin. And there is no consensus on this today. One of the wilder theories, that the coconut palm has an American origin, is almost certainly wrong. Another theory holds that it originated in the islands of the western Pacific. More likely is that it was first cultivated by peoples of India or Southeast Asia, possibly Malaysia; emigrants from these countries then introduced the coconut tree to almost everywhere in the tropics of Asia and Oceania, assisted by the coconut's own dispersal and colonising ability, it being able to float in salt water for many months while remaining viable.

Cultural Uses: Like all Pacific Islanders, Fijians have a long and close association with this palm and have made full use of the tree often referred to as 'nature's greatest gift to man'. **Niu** is the universal name for the coconut amongst Fijians, but at least 11 varieties have been recognised in Fiji together with Rotuma:

Niu yabu (light coloured coconut) – tall palms with green nuts.

Niu damu (orange coconut) – tall palms with orange nuts.

Niu ni Toga (Tongan coconut) or **niu kitu** (coconut shell used as a water container) – tall palms with large nuts.

Niu drau or **buludrau** – a tall palm which bears a large number of very small nuts on each

The ubiquitous coconut *Cocos nucifera*.

bunch. They are used only for drinking, since they are too small and the flesh too thin for making copra.

Niumagimagi – a tall palm bearing large, elongated nuts which have a thick husk, favoured for use in making coir (**magimagi**).

Niuyabia – an uncommon tall palm, the fronds of which have distinctly drooping and clustered leaflets – **yabia** is the Fijian for arrowroot *Tacca* spp. Two of these palms are currently growing in Thurston Gardens, Suva.

Niu yalewa (female coconut) – an uncommon and unusual tall coconut, the inflorescence being unbranched, consisting of a single branch almost completely covered with female flowers, with only a small number of male flowers at the tip.

Niu Leka (short coconut) – groups of dwarf or semi-tall palms which tend towards early bearing – variable coloured nuts, although mostly green.

Niu ni Malea (Malayan coconut) – a dwarf coconut first brought to Fiji in the 1920s.

Rotuman – Tall palms with the reputation of bearing very large nuts but usually not heavy bearers.

Utogau or **Uta** (Rotuman name) – A palm found on Rotuma, Cikobia and in Lau. The husk is edible when chewed and has a sweetish taste, not unlike sugar cane.

Cultivation: Copra, the dried coconut meat (endosperm) from which is extracted coconut oil, remains the most important crop for all the Fijians of Fiji's smaller islands, and for many in coastal areas on the larger islands as well. The annual production of copra varies greatly, depending to a large extent on the world price – generally a reflection of the Philippines' crop. If there is a serious cyclone or disease in the Philippines, Fiji's copra producers quietly rejoice as the price will go up.

Fijians, of course, use the coconut for a myriad other things. Coconut oil (natural pressed product) has been used by Fijians since time immemorial as a skin balm for its soothing and healing properties. Only recently has it been found that all these properties are destroyed by the heat used in the modern industrial oil production process. Coconut cream is an essential and adaptable part of Fijian cuisine, while coconut leaves are used for everything from temporary mats to temporary hats.

Coconut trunks have long been used for rafters and beams in the Fijian construction industry and are now turned into high-priced furniture. The husk of the coconut provides a lasting cordage – coir or **magimagi**. The shell was used whole as a water container, or when halved it can be polished and used to dispense kava. It is an excellent fuel for the kitchen fire and more recently it has been found to make a high quality 'activated charcoal' and is also used as an industrial filter.

A distinctive coconut variant, *niuyabia*.

At least 12 coconut varieties have been recognised in Fiji and Rotuma, with variations in number, size, colour or nature of the fruit being major determinants.

But nothing is more important than **bu**, the world's most refreshing drink, the water from inside an immature coconut.

Conservation: No effective attempt has yet been made to ensure that all the Fijian varieties are maintained and not lost through the adoption of new hybrid varieties. Fiji is, however, a member of an international programme which is currently characterising and recording all the different varieties.

Metroxylon warburgii

Named for Otto Warburg, early German botanist.

Sago Palm

Description: Similar to *Metroxylon vitiense*, Fiji's endemic species. It is easy to distinguish only when in flower or fruit. The flowering stalk of *M. vitiense* is branched twice, while it is branched three times in *M. warburgii*. In addition, the fruit hang down in *M. vitiense* but are held erect in *M. warburgii*. The fruit of *M. warburgii* are pear-shaped while those of *M. vitiense* are round. More readily observable are the rows or 'combs' of spines on the underside of the frond, which tend to be less well developed and are arranged in relatively straight lines rather than the 'U' of *M. vitiense*.

Distribution: Indigenous in Vanuatu and the Santa Cruz group of the Solomon Islands. In Fiji it is an aboriginal introduction to Rotuma, and probably a more recent introduction to Viti Levu (near Sawani) and in several localities on Vanua Levu, where it is naturalised but nowhere in large numbers (refer distribution map under *M. vitiense*). It is most probable that *M. warburgii* in Samoa was brought from Rotuma as it is called **Niu Lotuma** (Rotuman coconut) there, either as an aboriginal or an early European introduction.

Habitat and Ecology: Grows naturally in similar wetland areas as *M. vitiense* but when planted may be found in any situation.

Cultural Uses: The sago palm is call **ota** by Rotumans, who are the most easterly people to use the palm for starch (**mar ota**). The Rotumans extract the starch in a similar manner to the Melanesians of Vanuatu, the Solomons and Papua New Guinea. They use it in a variety of ways – as a thickening agent for stews, a starch for clothes and it is also cooked directly, especially for the Rotuman delicacy **fekei mara**. Overall, however, the use of sago starch has been overtaken by the use of cassava and sweet potato.

Other uses of the **ota** include the use of thatch (**rau ota**) which is highly prized by the Rotumans, who consider this better than coconut frond thatch. Similarly, they prefer the **taufare**, a broom made from the leaf lamina, to those made from coconut. The immature fruits are eaten raw, after the thick skin has been peeled off.

Cultivation: An attractive palm which appears more compact and less rangy than *M. vitiense*. If tended, it grows well in high rainfall or well-watered locations and the very much less prominent spines are definitely a beneficial character.

Recent Introductions

Four exotic palms now naturalised in Fiji are relatively recent introductions, certainly since the mid-19th century, either for cultural use – *Areca catechu*; agricultural potential – *Phoenix dactylifera*; or as ornamentals – *Ptychosperma macarthurii, Pinanga coronata*.

Areca catechu

Genus from the a name used on the Malabar coast of India; species from a Malayan name.

Betel Nut Palm

Description: A tall, slender palm with a small, compact crown. The trunk is light green below the crown with prominent light nodes, becoming greyish below; it may grow to 20m in height and 25 cm in diameter but is usually smaller. The crown is small and crowded with arching fronds to 2m, erect bright green leaflets and a green crownshaft. The inflorescence emerges from below the crownshaft and is pale yellow when young. Tightly clustered egg-shaped and sized fruit develop and become bright orange when ripe. These are the well-known betel nut.

Distribution: In Fiji, this palm has become naturalised in only a few locations in the wet zone of Viti Levu and Vanua Levu, all close to villages or settlements, but it is widely grown elsewhere. It is not known where *Areca catechu* is native to, but this is probably Malaysia or the Philippines.

Cultural Uses: Chewing of a concoction based on betel nut is practised by millions of people in South and Southeast Asia across to the Solomon Islands. Fijians have never indulged, preferring instead kava *Piper methysticum*; however, a few Indians still chew betel nut but rarely, if ever, in public.

The betel nut is not chewed alone; the seed is extracted, wrapped in a fresh betel pepper leaf *Piper betel*, slaked or dried lime is added, and optionally a little tobacco. This is chewed for up to an hour and is a mild stimulant, with other reported benefits including a reduction in intestinal parasites, controlling of dysentery and aiding digestion. Less pleasant side effects are the intensive red-black staining of gums, lips and tongues and intense salivation, which in many places is spat out indiscriminately and leads to blood-red staining of public places.

This palm was introduced to Fiji probably in the 1860s by Solomon Island labourers as a source of betel nuts. To this day it is still unfamiliar to most Fijians, but descendants of the Solomon Island labourers have planted it in and around their villages, most notably their major settlement at Wailoku, near Suva. They no longer partake of betel nut (preferring the local brew kava), but are happy to allow visiting Solomon Islanders, such as University of the South Pacific students, access to their groves. The Fijian name for this palm, bua, was simply borrowed from Wai, the language of the Fiji Solomon Islanders, but this name is, like the plant, unknown to most Fijians.

Cultivation: Widely cultivated and used as a landscape palm in Fiji, as well as a favoured indoor pot plant. Also planted extensively by Hindus, it is an object of veneration in Fiji by some members of the Indian community.

Phoenix dactylifera

Genus from the Greek name for the palm; species name meaning date-bearing or finger-bearing.

Date Palm, Kajoor

Description: A robust, tall palm to 25m with a stout, gnarled trunk to 75 cm diameter, bearing the persistent frond bases, or the scars thereof. The crown comprises a large cluster of graceful, spreading fronds which are silvery-green in colour and grow to 3m in length. Withered fronds hang down the trunk. There is no crownshaft and the inflorescences, bright orange in colour, emerge between the growing fronds. Individual palms are either male or female. Numerous suckers grow around the base of younger individuals.

Distribution: Now common as a naturalised palm in coastal areas of Nadi Bay, especially at the mouth of the Sabeto River and Wailoaloa Beach on Viti Levu. Elsewhere it is likely to have been planted. This palm is native to North Africa.

Habitat and Ecology: A restricted naturalised range in Fiji in one coastal area with sandy soils on the drier side of Viti Levu.

Cultural Uses: No Fijian name recorded for this palm. An important economic plant, 'dates' have been an essential life support product for the peoples of North Africa and the Sahara Desert since at least 4000 BC. In Fiji this palm was introduced in the 1880s and since then has been planted as an ornamental and for its fruits. Tuvalu and Kiribati islanders staying in Nadi have, in the past, used this palm for the preparation of alcoholic 'toddy'.

Cultivation: A very hardy ornamental palm which is excellent for dry, sandy coastal areas, but is rarely used in landscapes in Fiji. Grows equally well in Suva and other wet locations, although it does not fruit well. May be propagated from seed or sucker.

Four recent palm introductions that are now naturalized in Fiji. Left to right:
Areca catechu, *Pinanga coronata*, *Phoenix dactylifera*, *Ptychosperma macarthurii*.

Pinanga coronata

Genus from the Malaysian *pinang*, a palm; species from the Latin *corona*, a crown. Formerly known as *P. kuhlii*.

Ivory Cane Palm

Description: A clumping palm with slender yellowish trunks to about 8m tall and 10 cm in diameter. The trunks are bright green with prominent rings and the fronds are scattered along the trunk, there being no specific crown. The bright green fronds have variable sized leaflet segments and a swollen crownshaft. The inflorescence first emerges at just above ground level below the crownshaft, creamy white when in flower; a cluster of small red fruit develop.

Distribution: Restricted to Coloisuva and Savura area outside Suva, especially under the now mature mahogany plantations there.

Habitat and Ecology: An understorey palm which grows well under complete canopy but can also survive in open sunlight, though it does not do well in such locations. This is a potentially serious invasive species, now completely dominating the undergrowth under the mahogany plantation past Coloisuva village and spreading through the Coloisuva Forest Park, Savura Forest Reserve and Savura catchment.

Cultural Uses: A recent introduction not currently recognised by Fijians.

Cultivation: Reported to have been brought to Fiji in the 1970s as an ornamental in a garden in Coloisuva. An attractive and potential landscape palm which grows very readily in Suva's wet climate; however, its invasive properties are serious and its use should be restricted to areas well away from native forest.

Conservation: A serious invasive species that requires attention. If it has the potential to spread through native forest in the manner it has colonised and dominated the Coloisuva mahogany plantations, then it has serious implications for the ecology of our native forest and attempts should be made to eradicate it, before this becomes impossible.

Ptychosperma macarthurii

Genus name refers to the unusual five-grooved seed; species named for Sir William MacArthur, New South Wales, Australia.

MacArthur Palm; Cluster Palm

Description: Characterised by its dense clustered habit with up to 10, perhaps more, suckers emerge from the base. Grows to 6-7m in exposed situations and up to 15m or more when grown under a canopy, with a green becoming blotched grey trunk to 15 cm in diameter. Attractive arching fronds with broad, dark green leaflets and light green crownshaft. A large inflorescence emerges beneath the crownshaft and when ripe are laden with a striking yellow, orange and red array of small fruit to 2 cm long by 1 cm.

Distribution: Found on the main islands, especially around Suva where it is occasionally very common in urban and peri-urban areas, but also out in farmland and old village garden areas. Occurs commonly along drainage lines, hedgerows, fences and in unkempt gardens. This species is native to northeastern Queensland, islands of the Torres Strait and south-central New Guinea, growing in areas subject to periodic inundation.

Habitat and Ecology: A fast-growing and hardy species, but has not penetrated forest to any significant degree. The main dispersers of its fruit are red-vented bulbuls *Pycnonotus cafer* and jungle mynahs *Acridotheres fuscus*.

Cultivation: An easily grown, hardy and attractive palm which can be grown in full sunlight, reported to be very responsive to nitrogenous fertilisers. Not a good pot plant unless placed in a full light situation. However, in Suva it is frequently attacked by a leaf-eating insect which gives its fronds a tattered appearance with white blotches.

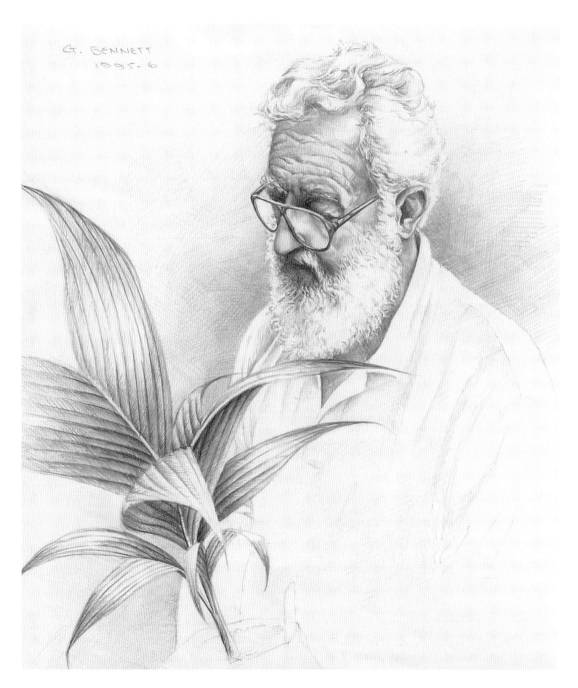

The late Dick Phillips, whose infectious enthusiasm and deep knowledge of Fiji's palms was shared with all. Portrait by George Bennett.

Propagation and Culture of Fiji's Native Palms

By Dick Phillips

Introduction (ed.)

Dick Phillips embraced the computer several years before his death and soon maintained excellent lists and a journal-like manuscript of his collection. This manuscript was given to David Zundel at the Garden of the Sleeping Giant and is the basis of this chapter. Dick's writing has been retained, as far as possible, although it has been edited for publication by the author who has also added the section on Collections, as well as a few observations which are identified by (ed.) at the end of the sentence or paragraph.

Dick was a very generous man who provided palms to all who he felt would look after them. He had personally planted an extensive collection of native palms on the University of the South Pacific campus and at Thurston Gardens in Suva, only to be dismayed at how poorly they were maintained. At the time of his death, he was actively assisting the Garden of the Sleeping Giant to establish Fiji's most comprehensive palm collection, and he had helped Dennis Beckmann (Korotogo[14]) and Robbie Stone (Pacific Harbour) build up their substantial collections, as well as the author's modest plantings at Tamavua.

Preparing Seed (ed.)

Fruit for seeds should be collected only when you are sure that it is mature. Usually some of the fruit will have already fallen to the ground. To prepare the seed, the fleshy outer portion needs to be removed. In most *Balaka* and the smaller *Veitchia* this is relatively simple and the seed can be easily extracted and the pulp cleaned off with a cloth. For other species, it may be necessary to soak the seeds for several days before cleaning the seeds with a wire brush or abrasive pan cloth. *Alsmithia* seeds are especially difficult to clean well.

When the seeds are clean of all material they should be soaked for an hour in a mixture of a good fungicide and a good insecticide. The seed is then placed in moist sphagnum moss, carefully labelled with name and date and placed inside a zip-lock plastic bag. Getting the right moisture for the sphagnum moss needs experience but in general you can thoroughly wet the moss and then squeeze as much water out of it as possible in your fist. The zip-lock bags can then go onto heated trays or placed in a location which is not subject to direct sunlight and keeps a relatively constant temperature, as close to 30°C as possible. The bags should be inspected weekly and if any fungus develops, the affected seed should be taken out, cleaned, resoaked in another fungicide and put into new zip-lock bags with new sphagnum moss.

---

[14] Since Dennis Beckmann's departure from Fiji, the fate of his collection is not known and it is not referred to in this chapter.

Palm seed is not famous for fast germination. While some of the *Balaka* and *Veitchia* can germinate in a couple of weeks, others such as *Alsmithia* and *Neoveitchia* can take several months and continue to germinate for several more months.

Species Accounts

Alsmithia longipes *(page 46)*

Seed Propagation: Ripe seeds germinate fairly easily if properly cleaned, but this is a difficult job. Heat is useful and germination usually begins within three months and may be spread over another three months.

Cultivation: The palms grow in wet forests so need good soil, good drainage and must never be allowed to dry out. Shade is essential for good appearance, especially in Suva at sea level. Two palms planted in the Botanic Gardens area of the University in 1988 continue to grow steadily but are clearly struggling as they are receiving too much sun. Inflorescences on these palms are atypical – far too short, they do not produce mature fruit and most inflorescences abort.

The palm appears to accept pot culture fairly well. I have not been able to get one into a really large pot but it would be well worth trying – if the palm could be exhibited with its brilliant red new leaf, it would be quite spectacular.

Collections: Dick Phillips distributed seeds and plants to quite a few people in Suva and some plants are known to be thriving. Also growing at the Garden of the Sleeping Giant, in Robbie Stone's collection and fruiting prolifically in the author's garden. Dick also ensured that seeds were distributed abroad and consequently it is now in cultivation in certain specialists' collections around the world.

Balaka longirostris *(page 50)*

Seed Propagation: Seeds usually germinate easily, in four to six weeks if mature. Heat may be helpful during cooler months. Seed, once cleaned, should not be allowed to dry out or viability is seriously affected.

The bifid leaves start to divide into individual pinnae when the palm is quite small. I also notice that the outer edges of the bifid leaves of this species show definite indentations which in time will be where the leaflets will divide – this seems to be quite different from other species in my collection. Could it be diagnostic? These indentations are not evident in the leaves once they mature.

Cultivation: Small palms are highly decorative, especially when showing the large terminal leaflets so common in *Balaka* spp. This palm grows in areas of high rainfall so must never be allowed to dry out. A good pot palm accepting surprisingly small pots. Usually grows only in very sheltered positions, although it does survive in the open where it may become ragged and wind-torn. Far more luxuriant in sheltered locations and believed to require well-drained, acid soil.

Collections: Very few in cultivation in Fiji. Currently grown at the Garden of the Sleeping Giant, the Stone collection and in the author's garden. Dick Phillips ensured that seeds were distributed abroad; consequently it is now in cultivation in certain specialists' collections around the world.

Balaka macrocarpa (page 54)

Seed Propagation: Seeds germinate easily and if properly cleaned in less than two weeks (ed.). As with *B. longirostris*, the bifid leaves start to divide into individual pinnae when the palm is quite small. *B. macrocarpa* shows signs of the indentations found with *B. longirostris* but not to the same extent.

Cultivation: This is a handsome palm with a full crown and relatively long fronds with broad leaflets. As this is sometimes seen as a semi-emergent in the wild, it is quite possibly tolerant of full sunlight, though likely to require shade when young and probably always requiring high rainfall (ed.).

Collections: No mature plants in cultivation in Suva, although those at the Garden of the Sleeping Giant are approaching maturity. Immature plants in the author's garden and others, believed to be this species in the Stone collection. No seeds distributed by Dick Phillips and as far as is known, not in cultivation outside of Fiji.

Balaka microcarpa (page 58)

Seed propagation: Seed usually germinates readily though some heat will speed germination in cooler weather. After cleaning, seed must not be allowed to dry out or viability may be affected.

Cultivation: The young palms have a striking appearance for the first few years as the juvenile leaves remain bifid and do not split until the trunk appears. They grow in an area of high rainfall so it is important not to allow the plants to become dry. It would remain as an understorey palm unless there was some clearing of trees. Occasionally a very old palm will become semi-emergent.

Collections: Very few in cultivation in Fiji. Currently grown at the Garden of the Sleeping Giant, the Stone collection and in the author's garden. Otherwise, believed to be but not confirmed in one or two specialists' collections around the world.

Balaka seemannii (page 62)

Seed propagation: When ripe, seed germinates quickly and easily, although heat may be useful in the cooler months. Seed should not be allowed to dry out after cleaning. I have found that keeping seed dry for even a week is sufficient to seriously delay or prevent germination. Seeds are produced by single palms and they readily germinate.

Cultivation: This is a hardy species which grows well in wet through to semi-dry forest but usually in good shade with free-draining soil, although it will grow in full sunlight (ed.). *B. seemannii* is a slender trunked palm and is very attractive when small. It would be acceptable for indoors but it would be necessary to keep humidity around the plants as high as possible.

Plants grow well in pots but it is best to keep the pots small. A good rich potting mix is best. In reasonably large pots, palms will flower and fruit – I have one palm in a 45 cm black pot which has been there for about 20 years, flowering, and fruiting regularly and now about 3 metres high.

Transplanting larger plants is not difficult, provided that the roots are not exposed and allowed to dry out.

Collections: Currently in cultivation in several locations in Fiji, but not as yet used as a landscape palm, something this small elegant palm could well become. Although in the past it has been reported as being commonly grown in Suva gardens, this is not the case – in fact no *Balaka* are commonly grown anywhere in Fiji. Grown commonly in Hawaiian collections and some specialists' collections elsewhere.

Calamus vitiensis (page 74)

Seed propagation: Nothing known, generally grown from seedlings which transplant quite easily (ed.).

Cultivation: This is an attractive palm in the right setting, but not likely to be a popular palm due to the dangerous thorns on the cirrus. Easy to grow given good soil and something for the palm to cling on. Shade is needed for young plants but larger plants do not transplant easily out of the ground – no problems for plants in bags.

Collections: A small colony growing at the Garden of the Sleeping Giant and another in the author's garden, where only three plants are currently flowering plants, all of which are male. Over a 13-year period, these three climbing palms which came as wild seedlings from Taveuni have grown to a length of 25-30m.

Clinostigma exorrhizum *(page 78)*

Seed Propagation: Seed is very small and is sometimes difficult to clean. Mature seeds usually take several months to begin germination which may continue for several months. Heat is valuable, especially in the cooler months.

Cultivation: Although growing naturally at high altitude (by Fijian standards), this palm seems to be adapting to growing at sea level in Suva. It has not been tried in the drier, western areas but I would expect that the higher temperatures and the low humidity would make growing conditions difficult. As this is a graceful, large palm I believe that it would be suitable in Suva and other wet areas as a street tree. The palm is not happy growing in a pot – even a large one.

Collections: In Fiji, growing only in the Stone collection, but in Hawaii is grown in several collections, where it is reported to be seeding well.

Cyphosperma tanga *(page 82)*

Seed propagation: Nothing known (ed.).

Cultivation: The major problem will be in acclimatising these higher altitude palms to grow at sea level where it is hotter and drier. At one time, Dick Phillips had about 20 seedlings from the wild of this form which were growing quite well in pots. Their eventual fate is not known (ed.).

Collections: No mature palms are known in cultivation anywhere in the world.

Cyphosperma trichospadix *(page 86)*

Seed propagation: Nothing known (ed.).

Cultivation: Nothing known (ed.).

Collections: As with *C. tanga*, this palm has not been cultivated in Fiji. However, a single fruiting palm is being cultivated in Hawaii by Jeff Marcus.

Cyphosperma 'naboutini' *(page 90)*

Seed propagation: Nothing known, although Dick Phillips recorded that Dennis Beckmann managed to procure seed by enclosing an inflorescence in a plastic bag, where the seeds germinated readily.

Cultivation: Plants from this *Cyphosperma* may succeed better than *C. tanga* at sea level, where it is hotter and drier. Transplanted seedlings survived and grew well.

Collections: Some immature palms are in cultivation in the Stone collection and in the author's garden.

Heterospathe phillipsii *(page 92)*

Seed propagation: Seed germinates readily with or without heat and often on the ground under the palm. The seedling leaf is pinnate as are subsequent leaves, making for a very attractive small plant. Growth rate fairly normal for palm seedlings – slow over the first year speeding up later. I have grown all my seedlings in some shade until they were about 1 metre high.

Cultivation: This is an attractive palm which could well be valuable as a pot plant for indoors as well as decorative in a small garden, although there is a tendency for the old leaves to remain on the palm for a period – regular cleaning might therefore be necessary. Although the young palms clearly need shade, adult palms can be fully exposed to direct sunlight. My large plant in the ground has been regularly attacked by insects in the crown and the leaves come out crippled. This requires treating with insecticide.

Collections: A few in cultivation in Fiji, with mature palms at the Garden of the Sleeping Giant, the Stone collection and in the author's garden. Described only in 1997; however, Dick Phillips had ensured that seeds were distributed abroad and consequently it is now in cultivation and fruiting in certain specialists' collections in Hawaii and elsewhere around the world.

Hydriastele boumae *(page 98)*

Seed propagation: Well cleaned seed germinates readily within two weeks and without heat (ed.).

Cultivation: Initially I had two plants in 60 litre bags which carried four leaves up to 4 metres long. These plants were only 10 to 12 cm thick at ground level where the base was slightly swollen, thinning down to 4 or 5 cm less than 20 cm above the soil. They required shade to grow well and it is important to keep these plants in an area sheltered from the wind as wind would easily damage the leaves and petioles. The young palms in the forest with trunks of 1-4m and very large bifid leaves are quite striking.

Collections: Seeds germinated in Suva are now thriving as three-year-old seedlings in the author's garden. Those planted out have done better than those in pots. These are the only known plants in cultivation.

Hydriastele vitiensis *(page 102)*

Seed propagation: Seed germinates quite readily. With some heat, it germinates after about two months and continues to germinate for a further two months.

Cultivation: Seedlings are fairly slow. The seedlings from seed in January 1995 are now starting to grow well though still in small bags – it would appear that at least 18 months is needed before reasonably fast growth can be expected. I have not had much experience with this palm but expect it will grow well if it is provided with plenty of moisture, good drainage and good soil. The soil in the area where it comes from is often quite heavy red clay, which could be rather acidic. Most of the palms we have found are in the open, though often choked with low shrubs and subject to quite harsh conditions – they have to force their way through the undergrowth. However, they appear healthy and in good condition.

With its characteristic silhouette, this is an attractive palm. Currently growing well in Suva, but as yet there are no mature palms and none has grown without shade when young. As it approaches maturity, this palm readily tolerates full sunlight. This is, however, a tall palm which requires plenty of space (ed.).

Collections: Very few in cultivation in Fiji and no mature palms. Currently grown at the Garden of the Sleeping Giant, the Stone collection and in the author's garden. Dick Phillips ensured that seeds were distributed abroad and consequently it is now in cultivation in certain specialists' collections in Hawaii and elsewhere around the world.

Metroxylon vitiense (page 108)

Seed propagation: Seed germinates readily, either cleaned or uncleaned (ed.).

Cultivation: The palm grows normally in swampy areas with poor drainage but it will grow well in any area that never dries out. In drier areas it becomes stunted. Forms a large, quick-growing and attractive palm but the spike-bearing fronds are a drawback (ed.).

Collections: Cultivated in many gardens in Suva and Pacific Harbour, as well as at some hotels and villages.

Neoveitchia storckii (page 112)

Seed propagation: Seeds can be variable in germination, even when mature and fresh. My normal method of germinating is to lay down a bed of rice husks under the shelves of one of my palm houses, lay the cleaned and treated (fungicide and insecticide) seeds on top of this and then cover with another layer of rice husks. If this is kept evenly wet, germination should commence after two to three months and may continue for several months. Heat would be useful during the cooler months. The large seeds are distinctive with thick 'fibres' around the broader end. These are absent in the seeds of *V. joannis*, the only similar sized seed.

Cultivation: These palms do not grow well in pots and it is preferable to plant them out into their permanent position as soon a reasonable size is reached. Good drainage, plenty of water and fertile soil help fast growth. The large leaves, undivided in juvenile plants, tend to damage easily in the wind, so some staking may be necessary.

This is a strikingly handsome palm with a heavy crown of fronds that bear broad dark green leaflets. *Neoveitchia* adapts well to cultivation in open sunlight, provided it has plenty of water, though the young palms benefit from shade (ed.).

Collection: Dick Phillips planted this widely in Suva and gave seedlings away to many people and organisations, though most of the institutions Dick assisted with plantings (Prisons, Lami Council, USP, Thurston Gardens) have now lost most or all of their palms. A healthy colony is established at the Garden of the Sleeping Giant and elsewhere fertile palms can be found at least in the Stone collection and in the author's garden. Seeds of the palm have been widely distributed to specialists overseas.

Physokentia petiolatus (page 118)

Seed propagation: Seed is slow to germinate and heat may help.

Cultivation: I have doubts that we shall ever be able to get this palm to maturity at sea level. Dick Phillips had great difficulty growing this species in Suva, eventually managing to grow one to about 40 cm, with three leaves plus a spear. Particular difficulty was experienced in the hotter summer months (ed.). The author managed to grow one to about 1 metre in height with stilt roots well developed, but it died when damaged by a falling branch.

Collections: Not known anywhere in the world. Although this is a very attractive palm and its stilt roots are a rare novelty, this is clearly a palm for dedicated and resourceful enthusiasts only.

Physokentia thurstonii (page 120)

Seed propagation: Nothing known (ed.).

Cultivation: Nothing known (ed.).

Collections: Not in cultivation anywhere in the world. A very attractive medium-sized palm with its well marked green trunk, prominent crownshaft and distinctive stilt roots. No attempts at cultivation of this species are known to the author, but since it is tolerant of low elevations in some locations on Vanua Levu, it may be hardier than *P. petiolatus*.

Pritchardia pacifica (page 122)

Seed propagation: Seed is available all the year and germinates easily with or without heat.

Cultivation: This palm is rapidly becoming more common in gardens in Fiji. While the palm grows well in good rich soils with plenty of water and humus, it will also accept the harsh conditions and alkaline soils of the resort islands off Nadi. It will grow in full sun as well as in some shade. In heavy shade the palm is much more open and less attractive. One mature and flowering palm in my garden sets very little seed. It is possible that this species is partially self-sterile, as groups of palms set seed readily.

This palm appears to be very susceptible to attack from mealy bugs, though they do not appear to do much damage. The palm is also susceptible to rhinoceros beetle attack which can be serious – the leaves can be badly misshapen and I have known of a mature tree being killed when the burrowing beetle hit the growing point.

Collections: Widely cultivated in Fiji and internationally.

Pritchardia thurstonii (page 126)

Seed propagation: Seed germinates readily with or without heat.

Cultivation: There are now fruiting trees at the Mana Island Resort (which I planted in about 1983) and at the approaches to Lami Town from Suva – these are plants which I gave to the Lami Town Council. They have had little care and attention and are regularly attacked by rhinoceros beetle. On Mana Island the soil is dry, sandy and alkaline (pH about 8.5) while at Lami the soil is heavier and more acid, though probably sandy near the harbour. The palms also appear to thrive on good, well drained, heavy soils in the wetter areas of Fiji but are less attractive when grown in heavy shade.

Collections: The Stone collection has palms from Dick's Mana Island seed. The author has a single fruiting tree from seed collected on Ogealevu in 1986. The centre of the driveway from the front gate up to Parliament was supposed to have been planted with this species with *P. pacifica* on either side. However, as the palms have matured it transpires they are all *P. pacifica*. The landscape contractor has long since returned to New Zealand!

Veitchia filifera (page 130)

Seed propogation: Mature seed germinates readily without heat and continues to germinate for at least six weeks.

Cultivation: These could be good landscaping palms as they seem to grow quite easily, and given just a little shade when small, they can develop into attractive medium-sized trees. The mature palms in their natural habitat commonly experience some sun although, naturally, they would be largely understorey palms, only breaking through the canopy at full maturity. The usual conditions needed for most *Veitchia* spp. are good soil, plenty of water in dry weather and some shade. This palm grows well in seasonally dry forest areas of Vanua Levu and is likely to be more tolerant than *V. vitiensis* (ed.).

Collections: The Garden of the Sleeping Giant, University of the South Pacific, Stone collection and the author all have this species in good numbers. Limited fruiting in a few specialists' collections internationally.

Veitchia joannis (page 134)

Seed propagation: Mature seed germinates quite easily with or without heat – though it is probably useful in colder weather. Germination starts after about four to six weeks and continues for several months. Seedlings can take fairly strong light once four or five leaves have formed but some shade is beneficial for fast growth. Seeds also germinate easily in the long grass under the trees.

Cultivation: These palms do not take well to growth in pots and much prefer being planted out into their permanent positions as soon as possible. As they come from areas of high rainfall the seedlings, and mature plants, must never be allowed to dry out. It is a fast-growing species which thrives in full sunlight, although when young it prefers a semi-shaded position.

On numerous occasions I have tried to use this palm in landscape work in Suva but there is the criticism that, when the palm is very tall, the head is small in proportion to the whole tree. I find this criticism rather strange, because although the palm is quite fast growing, it would be 15 to 20 years at least, before this stage is reached. Even then, if the palms are planted as a group their effect is very graceful and tropical.

Collections: This is an elegant and sought after palm which is now widely grown throughout the tropics, but surprisingly is rarely used as a landscape tree in Fiji, although there are quite a few widely scattered through Suva, usually as individual trees. Present in the Stone collection, a well-established colony in the USP campus and five palms in the author's garden.

Veitchia simulans (page 138)

Seed propagation: Seed, when available, is slow to germinate and heat appears to help. It may take four or five months for germination to begin and it is spasmodic over many months.

Cultivation: This is an attractive palm which would make a good garden subject provided that some shade, plenty of water, good drainage and good soil are available.

Collections: A single fruiting palm in Thurston Gardens and also present in the Stone collection. None known in cultivation outside of Fiji.

Veitchia vitiensis *(page 140)*

Seed propagation: Mature seed normally germinates in four to six weeks, with or without heat. Germination will continue for a month or so but seed which has not then germinated is best thrown away. Older seed which has been stored may take longer to germinate. There are no major problems in growing seedlings, though shade helps to maintain fast growth.

Cultivation: This is an attractive medium-sized palm which grows readily in full sunlight, though when young it prefers semi-shade. Although it is probably not drought-tolerant, it is surprising that it is not used at all in landscapes in Fiji. It grows vigorously in cultivation in Suva and fruits prolifically (ed.).

Collections: Present in the Stone collection; the author has a thriving colony in his Tamavua garden. In cultivation in Hawaii but not known from elsewhere internationally.

Notes:

Table 4: Summary of landscape characteristics of Fiji's indigenous palms

Species	Height	Frond length	Trunk Diameter	Trunk Colour
TALL PALMS (over 18m including foliage)				
Veitchia joannis	25m +	4m	25cm	Grey brown becoming very pale, almost white with age
Hydriastele vitiensis	23m +	2.5m	30cm	Grey brown
Hydriastele boumae	23m +	2.5m	30cm	Grey brown
Clinostigma exorrhizum	20m	5m	28cm	Grey brown with basal prop roots
Neoveitchia storckii	18m	5m	25cm	Pale grey
Metroxylon vitiense	18m	5m	30cm	Grey-brown, often with persistent leaf bases
MEDIUM PALMS (10-18m including foliage)				
Alsmithia longipes	10m	3.6m	10cm	Dark grey-brown
Heterospathe phillipsii	15m	4m	20cm	Brown often with persistent fronds
Pritchardia pacifica	10m	1.5m	20cm	Pale brown, fissured
Pritchardia thurstonii	10m	1.5m	20cm	Pale brown, fissured
Veitchia filifera	12m	3m	Usually 10cm but up to 20cm	Pale grey-brown

Note: most palms can vary greatly in height and foliage characteristics depending on their growing environment. Height is especially variable and dependent on the height of surrounding vegetation or the canopy above. The heights given here are considered likely heights to be reached in 'open' situations.

Fruit Colour & Size	Water	Sun/Shade Requirements	Other
Large fruit cluster with large, bright red fruit, 5cm	Hardy	Hardy, tolerant to full sunlight. Seedlings grow best in shade	Fast grower; excellent landscape potential
Large fruit cluster of tiny whitish fruit	Requires plenty of water	Mature palm tolerant to full sunlight. Seedlings grow best in shade	Seedlings grow slowly
Large fruit cluster of small yellow-white fruit	Requires plenty of water	Mature palm tolerant to full sunlight. Seedlings grow best in shade	
Large fruit cluster of tiny red fruit	Requires plenty of water	Mature palm tolerant to full sunlight. Seedlings grow best in shade	Generally a high altitude species, may adapt to sheltered, well watered sites at sea level
Large, attractive flower stalk and fruit cluster of large, 5cm, dull red fruit	Requires plenty of water	Mature palm tolerant to full sunlight. Seedlings grow best in shade	Palm with excellent landscape potential in wet or well watered areas
Very large terminal flower and fruit stalk to 3m. Large, 7cm, attractive 'scaly' fruit	Usually grows in swampy conditions, but may grow anywhere with a good water supply	Tolerant to full sunlight	Unpleasant spines around frond base. Flowers and fruits once before dying, reportedly about 15-20 years old
Large fruiting stalk, large fruit – 3.5cm; crimson; fragrant	Requires plenty of water	Best in good shade. Can survive in full sun but not happily	Grows quite fast, can mature in five years
Small scarlet fruit, 1cm, on a compact wispy stalk	Requires plenty of water	Tolerant of full sunlight, but does not do well. Seedlings require shade	Does well as a pot plant
Compact fruit stalk emerging outside the leaves; shiny purplish fruit, 2cm	Drought tolerant	Tolerant to full sunlight	Excellent landscape species; well known internationally
Compact fruit stalk within the leaves; shiny purplish fruit, 2cm	Drought tolerant	Tolerant to full sunlight	Prefers well drained alkaline soil; but used in landscapes internationally
Large fruit stalk with abundant small (2cm) yellow and red fruit	Relatively hardy	Seedling requires shade but otherwise tolerant to full sun	Excellent landscape potential; especially varieties from dry forests of Vanua Levu

Table 4: Summary of landscape characteristics of Fiji's indigenous palms (continued)

Species	Height	Frond length	Trunk Diameter	Trunk Colour
MEDIUM PALMS (10-18m including foliage)				
Veitchia simulans	12m	3m	15	Grey-green, lightening with age
Veitchia vitiensis	12m +	3m	15	Grey-brown, lightening with age
SMALL PALMS (<10m including foliage)				
Balaka longirostris	7m	2m	6cm	Variable dark, prominent nodes
Balaka macrocarpa	7m	2.5m	6cm	Dark green to grey, prominent nodes
Balaka microcarpa	7m	2m	7cm	Dark usually grey, prominent nodes
Balaka seemannii	5m	1.5m	5cm	Greyish, prominent nodes
Balaka streptostachys	?6m	3m	10cm	Dark green to grey, prominent nodes
Balaka 'bulitavu'	5m	1.5m	5cm	Greyish, prominent nodes
Cyphosperma tanga	5m	2m	15cm	Chocolate brown, with persistent frond bases
Cyphosperma trichospadix	6m	2m	8.5cm	Green-brown
Cyphosperma 'naboutini'	5m	2m	10cm	Grey brown
Physokentia petiolatus	6m	2m	12cm	Green with prominent pale nodes. Greying with age. Prominent stilt roots
Physokentia thurstonii	6m	2m	12cm	Green with prominent pale nodes. Greying with age. Prominent stilt roots
CLIMBING PALMS				
Calamus vitiensis		1.5m + 1m cirrus	3cm	Pale, usually covered in leaf sheaths

Fruit Colour & Size	Water	Sun/Shade Requirements	Other
	Requires plenty of water	Good shade required	
Large fruit stalk with abundant small (2cm) yellow and red fruit	Relatively hardy	Seedling requires shade but otherwise tolerant to full sun	Good landscape potential
Medium fruiting stalk, large fruit – 3.5cm; crimson	Requires plenty of water	Good shade required	Believed to require sheltered location with well-drained, acid soil
Large fruiting stalk, large fruit – 3cm; orange-red	Requires plenty of water	May be tolerant of full sun when mature	
Small fruiting stalk, small fruit – 2cm; orange red	Requires plenty of water	Good shade required	May be a very slow grower
Small (1.5cm), bright red and usually plentiful	Plenty of water required	Prefers light shade, survives in full sun	Fast grower. Does well as a pot plant
Large fruiting stalk, small fruit – 2cm; orange-red	Requires plenty of water	Presumed shade only	
Large – 4cm, orange-red. Small fruit clumps	Presumed plenty of water required	Presumed prefers full shade	
Small yellowish fruit, 2cm, on an emerging wispy stalk	Requires plenty of water	Good shade and high humidity required	High altitude species. Not grown at sea level
Small yellowish fruit, 1.5cm, on an emerging wispy stalk	Requires plenty of water	Good shade and high humidity required	Not cultivated in Fiji, probably same as above
Small purplish fruit, 1.5cm, on an emerging wispy stalk	Requires plenty of water	Good shade required	Growing well in Suva
Compact fruit stalk with shiny red-black fruit, 2cm	Requires plenty of water	Good shade required	High altitude species. Not grown at sea level
Compact fruit stalk with shiny red-black fruit, 2cm	Requires plenty of water	Good shade required	High altitude species. Not grown at sea level
Male and female palms separate, small clumps of 'scaly' white fruit	Requires plenty of water	Requires shade as a seedling but seeks the canopy quickly	Wickedly sharp rows of hooks. Can grow to 30m in length in 12 years

References

GENERAL REFERENCE

A recommended introduction to palms for the interested but non-specialist is:

Jones, D.L. 1995. *Palms throughout the World.* Reed New Holland, Australia.

IMPORTANT REFERENCES FOR FIJI'S PALMS

Ash, J. 1988. Demography and production of *Balaka microcarpa* Burret (Arecaceae), a tropical Understorey palm in Fiji. *Australian J. Bot.* 36: 67-80.

_____. 1992. Vegetation ecology of Fiji: past, present, and future perspectives. *Pacific Sci.* 46(2): 111-127.

Athens, J.S. 1997. Hawaiian Native Lowland Vegetation in Prehistory. In: P.V. Kirch & T.L. Hunt (Eds), *Historical Ecology in the Pacific Islands, Prehistoric Environmental and Landscape Change.* Yale Univ. Press.

Baker, W. J., Ross Bayton, John Dransfield and Rudi Maturbongs (2003). A Revision of the *Calamus aruensis* (Arecaceae) complex in New Guinea and the Pacific. *Kew Bulletin* 58: 351-370.

Baker, W.J. and A.H.B. Loo (2004). A Synopsis of the Genus *Hydriastele* (Arecaceae). *Kew Bulletin* 59: 61-68.

Balgooy, M.M.J. van. 1971. Plant geography of the Pacific. *Blumea* (supplement) 6: 1-222.

Beccari, O. & J.F. Rock. 1921. A Monographic Study of the Genus *Pritchardia. Memoirs of the Bernice Bishop Museum* 8.

Burret, M. 1928 Beitrage zur kenntnis der palmen von Malesia, Papua und der Sudsee. *Repert. Spec. Nov. Regni.* Veg. 24: 253-296.

_____. 1935. New palms from Fiji. *Occas. Pap. B. P. Bishop Mus.* 11(4): 1-14.

_____. 1940. Palmen and Tiliaceen von der sudsee aus der Sammlung des Bernice P. Bishop Museum, Honolulu, Hawaii. *Notizbl. Bot. Gart. Berlin-Dahlem* 15: 85-96.

Dowe, J.L. 1989. *Palms of the South West Pacific.* Palm and Cycad Soc. of Aust, Milton, Australia.

_____. 1991. The palms of Vanuatu and Fiji. *Mooreana* 1(1): 13-20.

_____. 1996. Regional priorities in Australia, the South-West Pacific Islands and New Zealand. In:

D. Johnson (ed), *Palms: an action plan for their conservation and sustained utilization*. IUCN, Morges, Switzerland.

_____ and P. Cabalion. 1996. A taxonomic account of Arecaceae in Vanuatu, with description of three new species. *Australian Syst Bot.*, 9: 1-60.

_____ and Y. Ehrhart. 1995. A new species of *Pritchardia* from Mitiaro, Cook Islands. *Principes* 39 (1): 36-41.

Doyle, M.F. and D. Fuller. 1998. Palms of Fiji-1. Endemic, indigenous and naturalized species: changes in nomenclature, annotated checklist, and discussion. *Harvard Papers in Botany*, Vol. 3, No.1: 95-100.

Ehara, H. and T. Mishima. 2003. Ecophysiology and Agronomic features of *Metroxylon vitiense* on Viti Levu, Fiji. Unpublished Report, Faculty of Bioresources, Mie University, Japan.

Essig, F.B. 1982. A synopsis of the genus *Gulubia*. *Principes* 26(4): 159-173.

Fuller, D. 1997. *Conservation Status, Diversity and Systematics of the Indigenous Palms of Fiji*. M.Sc. Thesis. University of the South Pacific, Suva.

_____. 1999. The lost palm of Fiji, a resolution of *Goniocladus*, and a preliminary cladistic analysis of *Physokentia*. *Mem. New York Bot. Gard.* 83: 203-212.

_____ and J.L. Dowe. 1999. A new species of *Balaka* from Fiji. *Palms* 43(1): 10-14.

_____ , Dowe J.L and M. Doyle. 1997. A new species of *Heteropathe* from Fiji. *Principes* 41(2): 65-69.

Garnock-Jones, P.J. 1978. Plant communities of Lakeba and Southern Vanua Balavu, Lau group, Fiji. *Bull. Roy. Soc. New Zealand* 17: 95-117.

Gorman, M.L. and S. Siwatibau. 1975. The status of *Neoveitchia storkii* (Wendl): a species of Palm tree endemic to the Fijian Island of Viti Levu. *Biol. Conser.* 8: 73-76.

Harries. H.C. 1992. Biogeography of the Coconut *Cocos nucifera* L. *Principes* 36(3): 155-162.

Kirkpatrick, J.B. and D.C. Hassall. 1981. The vegetation and flora along an altitudinal transect through tropical forest at Mount Korobaba, Fiji. *New Zealand J. Bot.* 23: 33-46.

Lucas, L. and H. Synge. 1978. *Neoveitchia storckii*. In: *The IUCN plant red data book*. IUCN, Morges, Switzerland. pp 413-414.

Mahabale, T.S. 1976. The Origin of the Coconut. *Palaeobotanist* 25: 238-248.

McClatchey, W. and Paul Alan Cox. 1992. Use of the Sago Palm *Metroxylon warburgii* in the Polynesian Island, Rotuma. *Economic Botany* 46(3): 305-309.

McPaul, J.W. 1963. *Coconut Growing in Fiji*. Dept. of Agriculture, Govt. of Fiji.

Milne, W. 1860. On the palms of the Feejee Islands, communicated by Prof. Balfour. *Trans. Bot. Soc.* (Edinburgh) 6: 358.

Moore, H.E. 1957. Synopses of various genera of Arecoideae: 21. *Veitchia*, 22. *Neoveitchia*. *Gentes Herbarium* 8(7): 483-540.

_____. 1965. The genus *Tavuenia*, Palmae-Arecoideae-Clinostigmeae. *Candollaea* 20: 91-102.

_____. 1966a. New palms from the Pacific. *Principes* 10(2-3): 85-94.

_____. 1966b. Palm hunting around the world VI. New Caledonia and Fiji. *Principes* 10(2-3): 114-130.

_____. 1969. A synopsis of the genus *Physokentia*. *Principes* 13 (4): 120-136.

_____. 1973. The major groups of palms and their distribution. *Gentes Herb*. 11:27-141.

_____. 1977. Endangerment at the specific and generic levels in palms. In: G.T. Prance and T.S. Elias (eds), *Extinction is forever*. NY Botanic Garden, Bronx.

_____. 1979. Arecaceae. In: A.C. Smith, *Flora Vitiensis Nova: A New Flora of Fiji*, Vol. 1. Pacific Tropical Bot. Garden, Lawaii, Kawai, Hawaii. Pp. 392-438.

_____, R.H. Phillips and S. Vodonaivalu. 1982. Additions to the palms of Fiji. *Principes* 26(3): 122-125.

_____, and N. Uhl. 1984. The indgenous palms of New Caledeonia. *Allertonia* 3(5): 313-402

Parham, J. W. 1972. *Plants of the Fiji Islands*, edition 2. Gov. Printer, Suva, Fiji.

Parkes, A. 1997. Environmental Change and the Impact of Polynesian Colonisation: Sedimentary Records from Central Polynesia. In: P.V. Kirch & T.L. Hunt (Eds), *Historical Ecology in the Pacific Islands, Prehistoric Environmental and Landscape Change*. Yale Univ. Press.

Phillips, R. H. 1993. Another new palm in Fiji. *Palms and Cycads* 30: 16-17.

____, and J. Dowe. 1995. *Neoveitchia storkii*: an endemic palm commemorated on a postage stamp. *Mooreana* 5(1): 26-28.

Seemann, B. 1862. *Viti: an account of a government mission to the Vitian or Fiji Islands in the years 1860-61*. Cambridge. (Reprinted in 1973, Colonial History Series No. 85).

_____. 1865-73. *Flora Vitiensis: A Description of the Plants of Viti or Fiji Islands, with an account of their history, uses and properties*. L. Reeve and Co., London.

Smith, A.C. 1950. Studies of Pacific island plants VI, new and noteworthy flowering plants from Fiji. *J. Arnold Arb*. 31: 137-171.

_____. 1951. The vegetation and flora of Fiji. *Sci. Mon* 73: 3-15.

_____. 1955. Phanegram genera with distributions terminating in Fiji. *J. Arnold Arb*. 36 (2&3): 273-292.

_____. 1979. *Flora Vitiensis Nova:* Vol.1. Pacific Tropical Bot. Garden, Lawai, Kawai, Hawaii.

_____. 1983-91. *Flora Vitiensis Nova:* Vol. 2-6. Pacific Tropical Bot. Garden, Lawai, Kawai, Hawaii.

Tomlinson, P.B. 1979. Systematics and ecology of Palmae. *Ann. Rev. Syst*. 10: 85-107

Uhl, N. 1982. Collecting *Alsmithia*: A last New Genus from Fiji. *Principes* 26(3): 138-140.

Uhl, N. and J. Dransfield. 1987. *Genera Palmarum*. The International Palm Society, Allen Press, Lawrence, Kansas.

Whistler, W.A. 1992. The Palms of Samoa. *Mooreana* 2(3): 24-29.

Zona, S. and Dylan Fuller. 1999. A Revision of *Veitchia* (Arecaceae – Arecoideae). *Harvard Papers in Botany* 4(2): 543-560.

Glossary

Bulbous   Bulb-like, expanded.

Cirrus   Whip-like extension of the leaf with barbed hooks as an aid for climbing i.e. *Calamus* spp.

Clustered   Clumping with several stems or suckers.

Crown   The head of foliage of a palm.

Crownshaft   A series of tightly packed, specialised tubular leaf bases which terminate the trunk of some palms.

Decumbent   Lying on the ground.

Dioecious   Bearing male and female flowers on separate plants (only Fijian species – *Calamus vitiensis*).

Distal   Farthest from the point of attachment.

Ecology   The study of the interactions of plants and animals within their natural eco-systems.

Endemic   Restricted to a particular country (also used for an island, region or area).

Endocarp   A woody layer surrounding a seed in a fleshy fruit; the innermost fruit wall.

Endosperm   Tissue rich in nutrients which surrounds the embryo in the seed.

Epicarp   The outermost layer of the fruit wall.

Exotic   A plant introduced from overseas.

Frond   Whole leaf of a palm (petiole plus the leaflets).

Frugivorous   Fruit-eating (generally referring to birds or flying foxes).

Genus   A taxonomic group of closely related species. Plural – genera.

Germination	The active growth of an embryo resulting in the development of a young plant.
Glabrous	Smooth, hairless.
Gondwana	Ancient landmass which included South America, Africa, Madagascar, India, Australia and Antarctica.
Habitat	The environment in which a plant grows.
Indigenous	Native to a country, island, region or area but not necessarily restricted there.
Inflorescence	The flowering structure of the palm.
Interfoliar	Between the leaves, those palms which bear their inflorescences between the fronds.
Juvenile	Young palms before maturity and flowering.
Leaf-base	Specialised expanded and sheathing part of the petiole where it joins the trunk.
Leaf scar	Node – site where fronds/leaves arose.
Leaflet	The lateral parts of a pinnate frond, also used loosely for pinnae.
Megafauna	Collective term used for a large number of 'giant' species.
Megapode	General term for the Megapodidae family of birds which are characterised by their habit of not incubating their eggs.
Mesocarp	The middle layer of a fruit wall.
Monocotyledons	The section of the Angiosperms to which palms belong and characterised by bearing a single seed leaf.
Monoecious	Bearing separate male and female flowers on the same plant.
Monotypic	A genus with a single species.
Naturalised	Exotic species now established and growing wild.
Node	A point on the stem where leaves or bracts arose.
Ovate	Egg-shaped in a flat plane.
Ovoid	Egg-shaped in a solid plane.
Palmate	In palms this refers to a circular or semi-circular leaf with segments radiating from a common point, i.e. *Pritchardia* spp.
Pedicel	The stalk of a flower.
Peduncle	The main axis of an inflorescence.

Pendant	Hanging down.
Petiole	The stalk of a frond (basal area without leaflets).
Pinnate	Once divided with the divisions extending to the midrib, usually referring to leaves/fronds.
Rachilla	A small rachis, the secondary and lesser axes of a compound inflorescence, the branch that bears the flowers.
Rachis	The main axis of an entire or compound leaf of a palm extending from the petiole to the end of the lamina.
Reins	Leaf fibres of palms, in particular referring to marginal strips that tie the developing leaflets together and subsequently hang down, conspicuous in some *Veitchia*.
Scale	A dry, flattened, papery body found on the young fronds and petioles of some palms.
Seedling	A young palm raised from the seed.
sp.	Abbreviation used for 'species', often when the species is not known. The plural is 'spp.'
Spathe	A large sheathing bract which encloses young inflorescences, often very prominent in palms.
Species	A taxonomic group of closely related plants, all possessing a common set of characteristics which sets them apart from another species.
Taxon	A term use to describe any taxonomic group – for example, genus, species.
Taxonomy	The classification of plants and animals.
Tomentose	Densely covered with short, matted soft hairs or scales.
Type	As in 'type collection' – refers to the collection from which the species was scientifically described.

Index

Entries in **_bold italics_** are Fijian, Rotuman or other vernacular names. Pages in **bold** indicate the start of Species Accounts.

A

Acridotheres fuscus 35, 157

adventitious roots 15

Agathis vitiensis 133

Alsmithia 8, 29, 33, 34, 35, 46, 49, 160, 161

Alsmithia longipes... 30, 36, 38, 40, **46**, 47, 98, 100, 161, 172

Andean wax palms..14

annular rings 15

Aplonis tabuensis 35, 98

Areca catechu 9, **153**, 155

Arrowroot 110, 148

Asia 74, 106, 146

Australia..................22, 29, 37, 74, 77, 138, 156, 180

B

Ba 137

balaka..53, 57, 61, 65, 70

Balaka 8, 17, 50, 53, 58, 65, 66, 69, 70, 71, 72, 160, 161, 162, 163

Balaka 'bulitavu'.. 28, 31, 37, 38, 40, 50, 57, 69, **70**, 72, 174

Balaka longirostris 8, 38, **50**-52, 69, 70, 161, 162, 174

Balaka macrocarpa.........8, 29, 31, 33, 37, 38, 40, 50, 54-56, 69, 70, 72, 90, 162, 174

Balaka microcarpa...............8, 31, 32, 37, 38, **58**, 59, 60, 69, 90, 162, 174

Balaka pauciflora 61

Balaka seeds..69

Balaka seemannii .. 8, 30, 38, 40, **62**-65, 69, 70, 98, 163, 174

Balaka 'natewa' 72

Balaka streptostachys............. 8, 28, 31, 37, 38, 40, **66**-70, 174

balakwa...53

Barking pigeon...34, 98

Bau 137

belaka..53

Beqa..39, 137, 143

Betel nut palm... 9, **153**

Betel pepper leaf...153

Bismarck Archipelago.................................29, 116

bitter palm 137

Blue-crowned lory 129

Bonin Islands 78

Bouma 11, 30, 38, 39, 49, 97, 98, 100, 101

Bouma National Heritage Park 49, 98, 138

_bu_...151

bua...154

Bua 77, 133, 137

buludrau...146

C

cagicagi 133

cagicake...133

Cakaudrove....................57, 77, 81, 105, 120, 133, 137

Calamus 8, 29, 74, 77, 179

Calamus vitiensis..................28, 30, 38, 74-76, 98, 163, 174

Caroline Islands 106

Carpentaria 138

cassava 151

Ceroxylon 14

Cikobia 148

cirrus 76, 163, 179

Clinostigma 35, 78

Clinostigma exorrhizum 8, 24, 28, 29, 30, 38, 40, **78**-80,
    98, 118, 164, 172

Cloud forest 24

Cluster palm 156

Coastal Strand Vegetation 26

Coconut palm 28, 146

Cocos nucifera 9, **146**, 147

Code of Logging Practice 37

coga 108

Collared lory 129

Coloisuva 28, 38, 39, 59, 61, 156

Coloisuva Forest Park..........................38, 59, 61, 156

Columba vitiensis 34

Conservation 37

Conservation Threat Status 40

Cook Islands 122

Copra 30, 148

Crimson-crowned fruit-dove 34

crown 15

crownshaft..15

Cyphosperma 8, 29, 33, 46, 82, 164

Cyphosperma 'naboutini' 28, 31, 37, 38, **89**-91, 164,174

Cyphosperma tanga......... 30, 31, 37, 38, **82**, 83, 90, 164, 174

Cyphosperma trichospadix...... 30, 31, 38, **86**-88, 90, 164, 174

Cyrtandra 22

D

dakua..133

Dama 77

damu..26, 81, 118

Date palm **154**

Deciduous Coastal Dry Forest......................................25

Degeneriaceae 23

Des Voeux Peak 79

Deuba 95, 110, 111

dispersers of palm seeds 34

Disturbed Vegetation 26

dora 137

Drokavia 81

Dromodromo Creek 84

Dry Forest 24

Ducula 34

dysentery 153

E

Environmental Impact Assessment 37

'Eua..21, 122

Evergreen Dry Forest 24

F

fakamalu..125

fakmaru..125

fekei mara 151

Fiji fan palm..122,125

Fiji flying fox..35

Fiji white-eye..35

Flora vitiensis..22, 46, 62, 178

Flora Vitiensis Nova 22

French Polynesia 29

Freshwater Wetland Vegetation 26

Friendly ground-dove..34

frond 15

fruit bats..35

G

Gallicolumba stairii..34

Gallus gallus..34

Galoa 105, 107, 108, 111

Garden of the Sleeping Giant................4, 43, 160, 161, 162,
    163, 165, 166, 167, 169

Gau 30, 34, 38, 39, 81, 117, 118, 137

Golden dove..34

Gondwana 21
Goniocladus petiolatus 28, 116
Gronophyllum 96
Gulubia 96
Gulubia microcarpa 102

H

Hawaii 29, 125, 129, 164, 165, 166, 170, 178
Hawaiian Islands 122
Heterospathe 8, 29, 35, 92
Heterospathe phillipsii 28, 31, 38, 92-94, 164, 172
Hydriastele 8, 10, 11, 17, 29, 96, 98
Hydriastele boumae 11, 28, 30, 31, 34, 35, 39, 97, **98**-101, 104, 165, 172
Hydriastele vitiensis 17, 29-31, 35, 37, 39, 40, 90, 96, 98, **102**-104, 165, 172

I

India 146, 153, 180
Indonesia 92
infloresence 15
intestinal parasites 153
irimasei 125
Island thrush 35, 118
IUCN Red List 41, 42
iviu 125
Ivory Cane Palm 9, **156**

J

Japan...78, 177
Jungle fowl...34
Jungle mynah 32, 35, 157

K

Kadavu.............................20, 34, 35, 39, 137, 143
kaivatu..143
Kajoor 154
karst 20, 33, 75, 137

kava...4, 148, 153
Keiyasi 137
Kiribati 154
Koro 34, 137
Koroyanitu Heritage Park 39
kula 129
Kumi...137

L

Lalage maculosa 35
Lami 167, 168
Lau 2, 20, 125, 127, 129, 137, 148
Lautoka 137
leaf scars 15
leva 129
levavatu 129
levawai 129
Levuana moth 30
Lilliput palm 14
Lomaiviti 137
Lowland Rainforest 23

M

MacArthur Palm 9, 156
Macuata 131
magimagi 148
Malaysia 146, 153
Mana Island 168
Mangrove Forest 25
Many-coloured fruit-dove 34
mar ota 151
masei 125
Matani Creek 57, 66
Matuku 137
meke...53, 65
meke wesi 125
Metroxylon....................4, 8, 9, 29, 33, 34, 106, 110, 146
Metroxylon vitiense.................30, 37, 39, 106-**108**, 109, 151, 152, 166, 172

Metroxylon warburgii 28, 106, 108, **151**

Micronesia 92

Moala 137

Monasavu 81, 118

Montane Forest 24

moto 53

Moturiki 137

Mt Delaco 118

Mt Koroturaga 97,98

Mt Mariko 86

Mt Sorolevu 40, 41, 49, 57, 66, 67, 70, 105, 120

Mt Nakobolevu 105

Mt Tomaniivi 21, 30, 83, 84, 118

N

Naboutini 90, 91, 103

Nabukavesi Creek 55, 57, 72

Nadarivatu 30, 118

Nadi Bay 154

Nadroga 84, 125, 137

Naitasiri 137

Nakauvadra Range 118

Nakavu 95

Nakobo 77

Namaqumaqua 4, 90

Namosi 57, 77, 81, 141

Namuka 137

Naqali 113, 115

Natewa 57, 63, 72, 73, 125, 137

Navai 84

Navonu 73

Navosa 53, 84, 137

Navua 26, 95, 105, 108

Navua River gorge 108

Neoveitchia 8, 29, 33, 34, 35, 36, 112, 115, 161, 167

Neoveitchia storckii 30, 31, 39, **112**-114, 166, 172

nesi 133

New Caledonia 22, 29, 82

New Guinea 22, 29, 74, 77, 92, 106, 110, 151, 157

niu 108, 143, 146

niu damu 146

niu drau 146

niu kitu 146

niu leka 148

niu Lotuma 151

niu ni Malea 148

niu ni Toga 146

niu yabia 149

niu yabu 146

niu yalewa 148

niumagimagi 148

niuniu 53, 57, 81, 95, 120, 133, 137, 143

niuniu 24, 98, 105

niuroro 137

niusawa 81, 137, 138

niusoria 108

niuyabia 148

nodes 15

Norway rat 32, 33

Notopteris macdonaldii 35

Nukurua 95, 115

O

Oceania...29, 146

Ogea 2, 33, 39, 127, 129

Orange dove.....................................34, 98

ota 151

Ovalau 29, 34, 39, 61, 108, 120, 137, 143

P

Pacific blossom bat 35

Pacific flying fox 35, 36

Pacific Harbour 160, 166

Pacific pigeon 34

palm heart 95, 105, 110

Papua 29, 74, 92, 110, 151

persistent leaf 15, 76, 154, 172, 174

petiole 15

Philippines 92, 148, 153

Phillips, Dick 4, 7, 9, 10, 43, 81, 84, 92, 93, 100, 158, 159, 160, 162, 164, 165, 166, 167

Phoenix dactylifera 9, 153, **154**, 155

Phygis solitarius 129

Physokentia 8, 29, 116, 126

Physokentia petiolatus 30, 35, 39, 116-**118**-120, 167, 174

Physokentia rosea 28, 116, 118

Physokentia thurstonii 30, 39, 40, 98, 116, **120**, 121, 167, 174

Pinanga coronata 9, 28, 32, 153, 155, **156**

Piper betel 153

Piper methysticum 153

piu 125

Polynesia 122, 125, 129

Polynesian rat 32, 33, 129

Polynesian starling..35, 98

Polynesian triller 35

Pritchardia 2, 4, 9, 29, 122, 125, 137, 172, 180

Pritchardia pacifica 4, 16, 28, 29, 39, **122**-126, 128, 129, 167, 168, 172

Pritchardia seeds 129

Pritchardia thurstonii 31, 33, 39, 43, **126**-129, 168

prop roots 15, 78, 172

Prosopeia...................................32, 33, 35, 56, 57

Prosopeia tabuensis 34

Prosopeia personata 34

protected area 40, 42

Proto Oceanic 110

Psychotria...22

Pteralopex 35, 49

Pteropus 35, 36, 49

Ptilinopus layardi 34

Ptilinopus luteovirens..34

Ptilinopus perousii 34

Ptilinopus porphyraceus..34

Ptilinopus victor 34

Ptychosperma macarthurii.................. 9, 32, 35, 153, 155, **156**

Pycnonotus cafer 32, 35, 157

Q

Qamea 77

qanuya 77

qavio 81

qavio damu 81

Queensland 77, 157

R

Rainfall – isohyetal map of Vanualevu and Taveuni 21

Rainfall – isohyetal map of Vitilevu....................................20

Rainforest Vegetation 23

Rairaimatuku Plateau 24, 30, 118

rambia 110

rats 32, 33, 36

rattan 14, 77

Rattus exulans 33, 129

Rattus norvegicus 33

Rattus rattus..33

rau ota 151

Ravilevu Nature Reserve...138

Red List..41, 42

red palm 137

Red-vented bulbul..32, 35, 157

reins 15, 134, 143

Rewa delta...108, 110, 137

Rewa River 115

rhinoceros beetle 30, 115, 168

River Vegetation 26

Rokosalase 131

roro 125, 137

rosea 116

Rotuma............108, 110, 120, 122, 125, 146, 148, 150, 151

S

Sabeto River 154

Sago palm 4, 9, 42, **108**, 110, 111, 146, **151**

sagu 108

Sahara Desert 154

sakiki 125, 137, 143

Samoa 29, 50, 78, 106, 122, 151

Samoan flying fox..35

Santa Cruz 151

saqiwa 137

Satulaki village 70

Savura Creek 61, 156

Savura Forest Reserve 61, 156

Savura Watercatchment Reserve......................................61

Savusavu 108

Secondary Forest 27

Serua 90, 105, 111, 137

Shining parrot 32, 33, 34, 35, 36, 56, 57, 95, 108

ship rat 32, 33

Sigatoka Valley 137

Silvereye 35

Siphokentia 96

soga 108, 110, 111

Solomon Islanders...110, 153, 154

Solomon Islands 29, 74, 77, 92, 106, 110, 116, 122, 151, 153

Somosomo 87

Soqulu..47, 98

soria 108

Sote 137

South-east Asia 29, 74, 106, 146, 153

Sovu islets 2, 33, 129

spathe..15

spear leaf 15

Sri Lanka 74, 96

Standard Fijian spelling..17

stilt roots 15, 118, 120, 167, 174

Stone collection...................162, 164, 165, 166, 167, 168, 169, 170

sugar cane...148

Suva 2, 5, 7, 11, 58, 59, 92, 105, 120, 148, 153, 154, 156, 157, 160, 161, 162, 163, 164, 165, 166, 167, 168, 169, 170, 174

sweet potato 151

Syagrus lilliputiana..14

T

Tacca leontopetaloides..110

tagadanu 118

Tagimoucia 86, 87

Talasiga Grasslands 26

Tamavua 10, 61, 160, 170

tana 118

taqa...118

taqwa 84, 118, 137

taufare 151

Taunovo Bay..108

Taveuni..........20, 42, 47, 77, 79, 86, 87, 97, 100, 101, 120, 137- 139, 163

Taveuni Forest Reserve............................38, 39, 138

Taveunia 82

Thurston Gardens............................120, 148, 160, 167, 169

tobacco 153

toddy...154

Tomaniivi Nature Reserve.........................38, 39, 118

Tonga 21, 122, 130

Tongan coconut..146

torau 137

Torres Strait..157

Totoya 137

tropical rainforest 29

Turdus poliocephalus 35, 118

Tuvalu 154

U

U.S. Exploring Expedition 61

Uea 28, 122

University of the South Pacific 160, 167, 169

Upland Rainforest..24

Uta 148

Utogau 148

V

Vago Forest Reserve 61

Valaga Bay 108

Vanuabalavu 2, 33, 39, 129, 137

Vanuatu 29, 74, 77, 82, 92, 106, 110, 112, 116, 122, 130, 138, 151

Vatuvonu 120, 121, 133

Veitchia 17, 28, 130, 143, 160, 169

Veitchia filifera................................... 9, 17, 30, 34-36, 39, 40, **130**-132, 138, 143, 168, 172

Veitchia joannis......................... 9, 17, 29, 30, 33-36, 39, 84, **134**-136, 143, 166, 169, 172

Veitchia pedionoma 130

Veitchia petiolata...130

Veitchia sessilifolia 130

Veitchia simulans 9, 17, 35, 39, 98, 130, 138, 139, 143, 169, 174

Veitchia vitiensis................9, 17, 29, 32, 34, 35, 39, 130, 133, 138-140-143, 169, 170, 174

Verata 137

Vidawa...98, 100, 101, 139

vilaito...115

Vini australis...129

viu 125

Vugalei...137

Vulaga..2, 33, 39, 43, 129

vuleito...115

Wai 154

Waidina 77

Wailoaloa Beach...154

Wailoku 153

Wailotua 75, 77

Wainibuka 77

Wainika 30, 81, 105

Wainimala..53, 77, 137

Waisoi 81

Waivaka 141

warusi 77

wataburaitaci..77

wataburakitaci...77

watabureitaci..77

Western Polynesia 129

Whistling dove 34

White-throated pigeon 34

yabia..110, 111, 148

Yasawa Group 137

Zosterops explorator 35

Zosterops lateralis......................................35

W

Wabu Reserve 118

Y

Z

Notes: